T0228226

Principles of Blended Learning

Issues in Distance Education

Series editor: George Veletsianos

Selected Titles in the Series

Principles of Blended Learning

Shared Metacognition and Communities of Inquiry

Norman D. Vaughan, Deborah Dell,
Martha Cleveland-Innes, and D. Randy Garrison

 AU PRESS

Copyright © 2023 Norman D. Vaughan, Deborah Dell, Martha Cleveland-Innes, and D. Randy Garrison

Published by AU Press, Athabasca University
1 University Drive, Athabasca, AB T9S 3A3

https://doi.org/10.15215/aupress/9781771993920.01

Cover design by Jessica Tang
Printed and bound in Canada

Library and Archives Canada Cataloguing in Publication

Title: Principles of blended learning : shared metacognition and communities
   of inquiry / Norman D. Vaughan, Deborah Dell, Martha Cleveland-Innes,
   and D. Randy Garrison.
Names: Vaughan, Norman D., 1960– author. | Dell, Deborah, author. |
   Cleveland-Innes, Martha, 1956– author. | Garrison, D. R. (D. Randy), 1945–
   author.
Series: Issues in distance education series.
Description: Series statement: Issues in distance education series | Includes
   bibliographical references.
Identifiers: Canadiana (print) 20230496709 | Canadiana (ebook) 20230496733
   | ISBN 9781771993920 (softcover) | ISBN 9781771993944 (EPUB) |
   ISBN 9781771993937 (PDF)
Subjects: LCSH: Blended learning.
Classification: LCC LB2395.7 .V38 2023 | DDC 371.3—dc23

We also acknowledge the financial assistance provided by the Government of
Alberta through the Alberta Media Fund.

Canadä   Alberta
            Government

This publication is licensed under a Creative Commons licence,
Attribution–Noncommercial–No Derivative Works 4.0 International: see
www.creativecommons.org. The text may be reproduced for non-commercial
purposes, provided that credit is given to the original author. To obtain
permission for uses beyond those outlined in the Creative Commons licence,
please contact AU Press, Athabasca University, at aupress@athabascau.ca.

This book is dedicated to our families, who supported our work on this text.

Contents

Principles of Blended Learning

Introduction

The aftermath of the COVID-19 pandemic and the resulting widespread adoption of blended and online learning have necessitated a rapid and radical rethinking of the teaching-learning transaction. The pandemic resulted in a forced test of the potential of blended and online learning. The possibilities and constraints associated with these approaches to learning were put to the test unfairly in many ways since many educators lacked a research-based framework to guide the redesign of their courses and programs.

The key was to provide guidance and support to educators to migrate their curriculums and activities to an online learning environment. The enormity of this challenge and the associated time constraints quickly became apparent. The tragedy was that faculty were too often left to their own devices or simply offered superficial teaching tips without a coherent understanding of the possibilities of an effective teaching-learning transaction online. Opportunities for both social and cognitive presence needed to be developed to facilitate effectively interpersonal relationships and intellectual discourse.

In this confusion, the Community of Inquiry (CoI) framework (Garrison, 2017) attracted considerable attention. This framework offered a coherent representation of and approach to online learning. For this reason, educators have turned to the CoI framework to provide perspective and guidance (Chiroma et al., 2021; Smadi et al., 2021a). The CoI framework has been a widely studied and adopted framework for blended and online education (Yu & Li, 2022). Considering the rapid developments in learning online, there is a growing need for a theoretical grounding of approaches and practices. In this regard, the CoI framework provides a map and rationale to rethink and migrate teaching and learning online. We need to look beyond technology and focus on the pedagogical assumptions and principles of practice associated with collaborative online learning.

We believe that the way forward is to adopt blended face-to-face and online learning. To us, this is the most obvious path to the acceptance and adoption of online learning. Blended learning (BL) is not new and has gained significant traction in higher education. We argued more than a decade ago that blended learning "is emerging as the organizing concept in transforming teaching and learning while preserving the core values of higher education" (Garrison & Vaughan, 2008, p. 143). This was based upon the ability to fuse the distinct capabilities of synchronous and asynchronous communication shaped by the CoI framework. Research has strongly supported this argument (Kintu et al., 2017). Moreover, the reality is that most classrooms in higher education have adopted BL approaches (Graham, 2019; Johnson, 2019). In addition, such approaches resonate with faculty when they understand the educational possibilities. The flexibility of BL approaches provides distinct advantages for teachers as well as students. Interestingly, as "blended learning" becomes the norm in higher education, the term itself is becoming moot as most traditional classrooms integrate online and face-to-face learning to various degrees.

The focus of this book is on the practical application of the CoI framework to the design, facilitation, and direction of blended courses and programs in higher education. We are guided in this quest by our previous books, *Blended Learning in Higher Education* (Garrison

& Vaughan, 2008) and *Teaching in Blended Learning Environments* (Vaughan et al., 2013).

In our first book, we defined blended learning as "the organic integration of thoughtfully selected and complementary face-to-face and online approaches and technologies" (Garrison & Vaughan, 2008, p. 148). We described how blended learning provides an opportunity to redesign fundamentally how we approach teaching and learning in ways that institutions of higher education might benefit from increased efficacy, convenience, and efficiency. In our second book, we provided further guidance on the design, facilitation, and direction of a blended course or program by using the following seven principles derived from the teaching presence sphere of the CoI framework (Vaughan et al., 2013, p. 17):

- Plan for the creation of open communication and trust.
- Plan for critical reflection and discourse.
- Establish community and cohesion.
- Establish inquiry dynamics (purposeful inquiry).
- Sustain respect and responsibility.
- Sustain inquiry that moves to resolution.
- Ensure that assessment is congruent with intended processes and outcomes.

Feedback from the publication of our previous books indicated that the unique feature of our work was the provision of a coherent framework in which to explore the transformative concept of blended learning. This book builds upon our previous work with an increased focus on designing, facilitating, and directing collaborative blended learning environments by emphasizing the concept of shared metacognition. Garrison (2018) describes shared metacognition as the awareness and management of one's learning in the process of constructing meaning and creating understanding associated with self and others. More specifically, Garrison and Akyol (2015a, p. 68) define the shared metacognition construct as including "two interdependent elements: self and co-regulation of cognition . . . [each exhibiting] a monitoring (awareness) and a managing (strategic action) function."

Content and Organization

This book begins with an overview of blended learning, the CoI framework, including the three overlapping presences (cognitive, teaching, and social), research related to shared metacognition, and how this concept is in dialogue with Indigenous ways of knowing. We then provide a description of how shared metacognition and the three components of teaching presence (design, facilitation, and direction) have been used to revise our seven principles of blended learning:

1. Design for open communication and trust that will create a learning community.
2. Design for critical reflection and discourse that will support inquiry.
3. Establish community and cohesion.
4. Establish inquiry dynamics (purposeful inquiry).
5. Sustain respect and responsibility for collaboration.
6. Sustain inquiry that moves to resolution and shared metacognitive development.
7. Ensure that assessment is aligned with learning outcomes and growth for all students.

The first two principles relate to the design and organization of a blended course. In Chapter 2, we focus on designing for relevance so that students have a sense of curiosity about and connection to the learning outcomes for a blended course. We provide design strategies and examples such as the creation of an online needs assessment survey, an online discussion forum to share experiences relevant to the course learning outcomes, the use of blogs and concept maps to help students set their own learning goals for a course, and design considerations for student group work.

Chapter 3, on facilitation, is connected to the third and fourth principles. Facilitation is the central activity in an educational Community of Inquiry for developing shared metacognition through the interactions among students and teacher. Facilitative actions, by "both the students and the teacher, create the climate, support discourse, and monitor learning. In the act of facilitation learners connect with each other, engage with the content, are cognitively present as intellectual agents, and carry out all actions central to the development and maintenance of the learning community" (Vaughan et al., 2013, p. 46). In essence, the teacher is responsible for modelling the growth and development of shared metacognition in a course by creating and sustaining constructive learning relationships. Creating a sense of community and collaboration is key to helping students develop their capacity for co-monitoring and co-managing their inquiry (i.e., shared metacognition). Unfortunately, studies indicate that many students in higher education have little formal experience working in groups (Chang & Brickman, 2018). This chapter provides activities and resources for helping students to learn how to work successfully in groups and to take responsibility for and control of the process of inquiry.

Chapter 4, on direct instruction, is not about lecturing. Direct instruction is about ensuring that students achieve the intended learning outcomes of a course or program and is related to the fifth, sixth, and seventh principles. It is an essential ingredient of any formal educational experience in order to help students learn how to learn by monitoring and managing their learning collaboratively (shared metacognition). It has been shown that students expect structure and leadership in higher education courses, and the roles and responsibilities for direct instruction should be shared by all members of a Community of Inquiry (Garrison & Cleveland-Innes, 2005). The focus of direct instruction is on rigour. In a higher education course, this can involve students in completing a challenging problem, task, or assignment that forces them to confront different perspectives and new ways of thinking. This process involves the teacher "nudging" the students forward in their academic studies (Thaler & Sunstein, 2008). For example, students are often content to share and discuss ideas with each other but require a "gentle nudge" to integrate and apply those ideas in course assignments and everyday life. This chapter provides examples, activities, and resources to create applied and challenging course assignments.

Chapter 5, on assessment, is related directly to the seventh principle. In a blended learning environment, diagnostic, formative, and summative forms of assessment can be integrated to support student learning. For example, this chapter demonstrates how pre-class activities can utilize diagnostic forms of assessment to help students gauge their prior knowledge and experience with course concepts. With regard to in-class (synchronous) activities, ideas are shared about how formative and peer assessment techniques can be used to explore and understand further the key concepts. Finally, we describe out-of-class (online) summative assessment activities such as the use of blog posts and video presentations to obtain feedback from external experts. The chapter also includes a section on evaluating the effectiveness of blended courses.

Chapter 6 highlights the type of collaborative leadership required to initiate and sustain an institutional blended learning program. The chapter provides examples of successful blended learning initiatives in higher education as well as a detailed description of how to use the CoI framework (Garrison, 2017) to design, facilitate, and direct a faculty development program for blended learning.

The Conclusion discusses next steps and future directions for applying the CoI framework to blended courses and programs in higher education by demonstrating how our seven principles of blended learning can be seen as in dialogue with Indigenous ways of knowing. There has been a shift from an individual to a more collaborative approach to learning (Kromydas, 2017), accelerated from our perspective by the COVID-19 pandemic. The historical ideal of education was to learn in collaborative Communities of Inquiry, which can foster the growth and development of shared metacognition (Lipman, 1991). The Maori of New Zealand refer to this concept as *ako*, which means to both teach and learn (Alton-Lee, 2003). *Ako* recognizes the knowledge that both teachers and students bring to learning interactions, and it acknowledges how new knowledge and understanding can grow out of shared learning experiences. Hattie and Yates (2014, p. 14) refer to this process as visible teaching and learning, "when teachers SEE learning through the eyes of their students and when students SEE themselves as their own teachers."

Conclusion

The primary audience for this book is composed of faculty and graduate students in higher education interested in quality teaching in blended learning environments. The secondary audience is composed of education technology professionals, instructional designers, teaching and learning developers, and instructional aides: that is, all those involved in the design and development of the media and materials for blended learning. Other audiences include higher education administrators, educational researchers, and government officials interested in issues of quality education. Although we focus primarily on blended learning in higher education, the collaborative constructivist principles here can be adjusted easily for application in the K–12 environment and the workplace.

1 | Conceptual Framework

An educational community of inquiry is a group of individuals who collaboratively engage in purposeful critical discourse and reflection to construct personal meaning and confirm mutual understanding.

—(Garrison, 2009, p.352)

With the pivot to remote learning during the COVID-19 pandemic, blended approaches to learning received an increasing amount of attention (Pelletier et al., 2021). Virtually all courses in higher education already incorporated digital technologies to some degree, and the pandemic accelerated this adoption. These technologies created new possibilities for students to interact with their peers, faculty, and content. The infusion of information and communications technology in higher education has drawn increased attention to the theory and practice of blended learning.

Blended learning inherently demands a fundamental rethinking of the educational experience and presents a challenge to traditional approaches to presentation. If we are to deal with the theoretical and practical complexities of rethinking the educational experience from a blended learning perspective, then the first challenge is to provide conceptual order that goes beyond rigid, non-reflective recipes. Such order and coherence are of particular importance to practitioners who might not fully appreciate the possibilities that new and emerging technologies present for engaging learners in deep and meaningful educational experiences. It seems to us that a conceptual framework might be of the utmost value to assist practitioners in navigating through the educational and technological levels of complexity.

This chapter describes blended learning and then establishes the rationale by which we can explore the practical challenges in implementing blended learning approaches in higher education. This rationale is operationalized in the Community of Inquiry (CoI) theoretical framework (Garrison, 2017). We outline that framework with a particular focus on shared metacognition and teaching presence. From this framework, we have derived the seven principles of blended learning. These seven principles provide the structure for this book.

Blended Learning

Since the publication of our book *Teaching in Blended Learning Environments* (Vaughan et al., 2013), there has been an increase in the types of and the terms for course modalities in higher education (Skrypnyk et al., 2015). Pelletier et al. (2021, p. 16) comment "that until recently higher education has, for the most part, been evolving its way forward—sometimes enthusiastically, sometimes hesitantly—in its adoption of online and blended course models." However, the COVID-19 pandemic significantly accelerated this evolution, forcing higher education to become inventive and create an array of new course models to cope with a truly unique situation. Especially challenging was the fact that many of the blended models crafted in response to COVID-19 had to be modified almost on the fly, according to the ebbs and flows of the pandemic. Pelletier et al. (2021, p. 16) indicate that "higher education now uses a wide and diverse spectrum of course models—so diverse, in fact, that the terminology can be confusing." Irvine (2020, p. 42) adds that "on today's higher education campus, there are likely a dozen new terms being used to describe different configurations around the modality of courses. Modality typically refers to the location and timing of interactions. What used to be a simple binary of face-to-face or online has now become so extremely complex that our ability to understand each other is impaired." In response to this confusion over nomenclature, a study conducted during the pandemic found that "students continue to want face-to-face classes more than any other learning environment, with a majority preferring either completely or mostly face-to-face" (Gierdowsk et al., 2020 "Key Findings" section). A research report on blended learning by Jooston and Weber (2021) also stresses a student preference for courses that combine face-to-face and online learning opportunities. The findings in this report were almost identical to those of a similar research study conducted in New Zealand (Brown et al., 2021) and those of another one in Australia (Cuesta Medina, 2018).

Johnson (2021) eloquently describes the importance of blending campus-based and online learning for students in order to prepare them for future life opportunities. In addition, Gordon (2021) emphasizes that institutions need to realize that "one size does not fit all," that each course or each program needs to find its own unique integration and balance of face-to-face and online learning in order to achieve student success and satisfaction.

This book retains the definition of blended learning that we put forward in *Blended Learning in Higher Education* (Garrison & Vaughan, 2008, p. 148) as "the organic integration of thoughtfully selected and complementary face-to-face and online approaches." By "organic," we mean that it is grounded in practice. By using the term "thoughtfully," we indicate a significant rethinking of how we should approach the learning experience.

With regard to a thoughtful approach, we expressly exclude enhancing traditional practices that do not significantly improve student engagement. That said, we do not want to restrict innovative blended learning designs by providing strict parameters for the percentage of time spent face-to-face or online. We have chosen to provide a qualitative definition that distinguishes blended learning as an approach that addresses the educational needs of the course or program through a thoughtful fusion of the best and most appropriate face-to-face and online activities. The key is to avoid, at all costs, simply layering on activities and responsibilities until the course is totally unmanageable and students do not have the time to reflect on the deeper meaning and engage in discourse for shared understanding. Twigg (2003) refers to this as the course-and-a-half syndrome.

Blended learning is the inspiration of much of the current innovation, both pedagogically and technologically, in higher education. By "innovation," we mean significantly rethinking and redesigning approaches to teaching and learning that fully engage students. The essential function of blended learning is to extend thinking and discourse over time and space. Higher education is fraught with considerable rhetoric about the importance of engagement. Still, most institutions' dominant course mode remains delivering content through either the lecture or self-study modules. Blended learning is specifically directed at enhancing engagement through the innovative adoption of purposeful online learning activities. The strength of integrating face-to-face synchronous communication and text-based online asynchronous communication is powerfully complementary for higher educational purposes.

The goal of blended learning is to bring them together in ways that challenge students academically, not possible by either mode individually. There is a distinct multiplier effect when integrating verbal and written modes of communication. An added benefit is that blended learning sustains academic communication over time. Moreover, students have time to reflect and respond thoughtfully. Finally, though there are significant administrative advantages in blended learning designs (e.g., access, retention, campus space, and teaching resources), the focus here is on the quality of the learning experience made possible through blended approaches.

In the next section, we explore the ideas of engagement and academic inquiry central to the ideals of higher education. These ideas are inherent to learning communities and provide the foundation for implementing blended learning. Learning communities provide the conditions for discussion, negotiation, and agreement in face-to-face and online environments with virtually limitless possibilities to connect to others and information. It is such a community that we describe next and that frames the principles that shape this book.

The Community of Inquiry Framework

An educational Community of Inquiry is a group of individuals who engage collaboratively in purposeful critical discourse and reflection to construct personal meaning and confirm mutual understanding (Garrison et al., 2022, "CoI Framework" section). The CoI theoretical framework was derived from higher education literature. It is a generic educational model applicable to any number of educational contexts and modes of communication. Although it has been used to study and design online educational experiences, it is just as applicable to collaborative and meaningful face-to-face inquiry. For this reason, it is effective in designing blended learning environments (Garrison & Vaughan, 2008; Vaughan et al., 2013). Moreover, the CoI framework is considered a pivotal contribution and turning point for distance education (Bozkurt, 2019).

The three key elements or dimensions of the CoI framework are social, cognitive, and teaching presence (see Figure 1.1). It is at the convergence of these three mutually reinforcing elements that a collaborative constructivist educational experience is realized. Social presence creates the environment for trust, open communication, and group cohesion. Cognitive presence has been defined as "the extent to which learners are able to construct and confirm meaning through sustained reflection and discourse in a critical community of inquiry" (Garrison et al., 2001, p. 11). It has been operationalized through the developmental phases of inquiry: triggering events, exploration, integration, and resolution. The third and cohesive element, teaching presence, is associated with the design, facilitation, and direction of a Community of Inquiry. It is the unifying force that brings together the social and cognitive processes directed to personally meaningful and educationally worthwhile outcomes. Research studies have demonstrated that a high level of teaching presence is a good predictor of

Figure 1.1

Community of Inquiry Framework

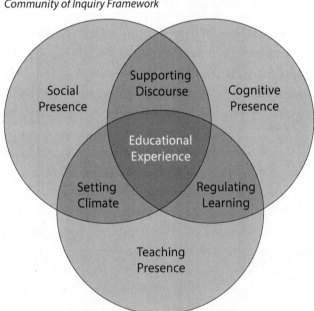

Note. From Vaughan, Cleveland-Innes, and Garrison (2013).

student success and satisfaction in a blended or online course (Shea et al., 2010; Torras & Mayordomo, 2011; Zhang et al., 2016; Zhao & Sullivan, 2017).

Shared Metacognition

As we have described, there has been an increased focus on the topic of student engagement and access to higher education. To address these issues, Littky and Grabelle (2004) advocate a curriculum redesign that stresses relevance, relationships, and rigour (the three Rs of engagement). It has been suggested that such a redesign would enable students to engage meaningfully in sustained learning experiences that can lead to a state of optimal flow. Csíkszentmihályi (1997, p. 9) defines "optimal flow" as "the mental state of operation in which the person is fully immersed in what he or she is doing by a feeling of energized focus, full involvement, and success in the process of the activity."

Recently, the focus in higher education has shifted from an individual approach to a more collaborative approach to learning (Kromydas, 2017). At the core of meaningfully engaged inquiry is the concept of metacognition, simply "thinking about one's thinking" (Chick, 2013, para 1). Metacognition is key to learning how to learn. It means increasing awareness of the learning process and taking responsibility for controlling that process (Garrison, 2017). Metacognitive approaches to learning start with understanding and engaging where possible in designing and planning the learning experience.

Consistent with this approach, Garrison and Akyol (2015a) have developed a shared metacognition construct integral to the CoI framework (Garrison et al., 2000). Shared metacognition exists at the intersection of the cognitive and teaching presence constructs of the CoI framework and goes to the heart of a deep and meaningful educational learning experience. We must therefore understand shared metacognition and its role in a Community of Inquiry. The following list provides a sample of CoI categories and indicators.

Elements	Categories	Indicators (Examples Only)
• Social presence	• Open communication	• Risk-free expression
	• Group cohesion	• Encouraging collaboration
	• Affective expression	• Emotions
• Cognitive presence	• Triggering event	• Sense of puzzlement
	• Exploration	• Information exchange
	• Integration	• Connecting ideas
	• Resolution	• Applying new ideas
• Teaching presence	• Design and organization	• Setting curriculum and methods
	• Facilitating discourse	• Sharing personal meaning
	• Direct instruction	• Focusing discussion

Source: Garrison et al. (2000).

In terms of understanding shared metacognition and its role in a Community of Inquiry, the premise is that developing metacognitive awareness and ability is core to becoming an effective inquirer. Metacognition generally has been accepted as consisting of two components: awareness of the inquiry process (monitor) and implementation strategies (regulation). Awareness allows students to monitor and manage/regulate actively the inquiry process. In short, metacognition awareness and implementation abilities provide the knowledge and strategies to monitor and manage effective inquiry. Most importantly, in a collaborative learning environment, awareness and implementation techniques are developed through critical discourse and the requirement of participants to explain and justify their thinking to themselves and others. The approach to developing a viable metacognition construct for collaborative learning environments

Figure 1.2

Shared Metacognition Construct

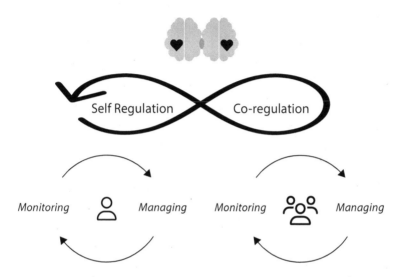

Shared Metacognition

Self Regulation   Co-regulation

Monitoring   Managing   Monitoring   Managing

is to subsume self and shared regulatory functions within a single construct. This shared metacognition construct (Garrison, 2017; Garrison & Akyol, 2015a, 2015b) reflects the dynamic dimensions of self and co-regulation, each exhibiting a monitoring (awareness) function and a managing (strategic action) function (see Figure 1.2).

To explore the practical implications of shared metacognition for a blended course, we need to begin with the construct of teaching presence.

Teaching Presence

Introducing a phenomenon as complex as teaching presence in a blended learning context is a daunting task. Beyond discussing teaching with technology, it requires explicating, examining, and describing a new approach to teaching in a new era of higher education. We see that changes needed in higher education are now emergent: "Neither the purpose, the methods, nor the population for whom education is intended today . . . bear[s] any resemblance to those on which formal education is historically based" (Pond, 2002, "Introduction" section). These changes include a new way of conceiving of and offering both teaching and learning.

We focus here on the teaching presence construct since evidence is growing that points to the importance of teaching presence for the success of a Community of Inquiry (Akyol & Garrison, 2008; Arbaugh, 2008; Eom, 2006; Shea et al., 2005; Taghizade et al., 2020). The conceptual framework that we offer requires new and expanded ways of thinking about the roles of teacher and student. Blended learning provides expanded possibilities and difficult choices for the teacher and students in a Community of Inquiry. Teaching presence is distributed but not diminished within the learning community since the importance and challenge are magnified in blended environments. Teaching presence is enhanced when students become more metacognitively aware and are encouraged to assume increasing responsibility for and control of their learning. Much attention needs to be focused on teaching presence if we are to create and sustain the conditions for higher-order learning.

The issue of shared responsibility suggests that each student in a Community of Inquiry must take on some responsibility for social, cognitive, and teaching presence. This is why the third element of the CoI framework is labelled teach*ing* presence and not teach*er* presence. It is not just the teacher who is responsible for social and cognitive presence issues. All students in a collaborative learning environment must assume varying degrees of teaching responsibility depending on the specific content, developmental level, and ability. From a cognitive presence perspective, the teacher and students must be prepared to clarify expectations, negotiate requirements, engage in critical discourse, diagnose misconceptions, and assess understanding. Students must also be aware of and active in social presence cultivation and ensure that all feel that they belong and are comfortable contributing to the discourse while simultaneously respectfully challenging ideas.

The pioneering innovation of virtual communication and community places both teacher and student in new ways of engaging, interacting, and contributing to learning. The challenge is that simply providing opportunities for interaction and collaboration does not ensure that students will approach their learning in deep and meaningful ways. The engagement of students in blended learning environments constitutes multiple roles and responsibilities. This multiplicity creates complexity since students must assume varying degrees of responsibility to monitor and regulate the dynamics of the learning community. This is consistent with the very nature of a Community of Inquiry with shared academic goals and processes.

Moving beyond the premise of shared responsibility, we must consider requirements embodied in the art of teaching in a blended learning environment. Teaching presence must be in the service of the learning objectives of the subject while attending to the needs and capabilities that students bring to the experience. However, the ways in which the role of effective teaching is crafted in blended learning environments are different and more complex. Our intention in this book is to create a clear picture of the role of effective teaching in blended higher education that will create the conditions for deep and meaningful learning. As this occurs, there will be shifts in terms of what is done in the community as well. As we illuminate and reconstruct the teaching process in higher education through the creation of blended learning communities, we must also examine the assumptions of teaching. This includes practices common to all teaching approaches in higher education, the new roles for teacher and student that emerge from these changes, the principles appropriate to the combination of teaching face-to-face and online, and the relevant changes to assessment strategies.

Principles

Principles are essential to translate theoretical frameworks into coherent practical strategies and techniques. Principles become even more valuable in coping with the complexities of integrating the potential of new and emerging communications technology. A principled approach to teaching that arises from a sustained Community of Inquiry takes us beyond the traditional lecture all too common in higher education. The principles that shape this book and give structure to teaching presence encourage students to assume greater responsibility for and control of their educational experience.

Collaborative constructivist approaches are more than interaction and engagement. The educational methods needed today represent purposeful collaboration to resolve an issue, solve a problem, or create a new understanding. The educational process outlined in this book is situated within the context of a learning community focused on purposeful inquiry in which students collaboratively assume increased responsibility and control to resolve specific problems and issues.

The seven principles that shape this book are derived deductively from the CoI theoretical framework. The principles are organized around the three sub-elements or categories of teaching presence: design, facilitation, and direction. For each of these three functions and areas of responsibility, we address the elements of social and cognitive presence. Considering the complexity of a collaborative blended learning experience, considerable care and thought must be devoted to design, facilitation, and direction. The following principles provide a guide to creating and sustaining purposeful Communities of Inquiry (see Figure 1.3).

The seven principles are as follows:

Figure 1.3

Seven Principles of Blended Learning

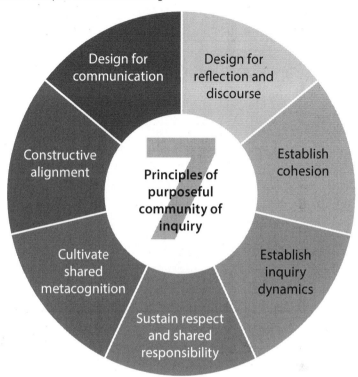

1. Design for open communication and trust that will create a learning community.
2. Design for critical reflection and discourse that will support inquiry.
3. Establish community and cohesion.
4. Establish inquiry dynamics (purposeful inquiry).
5. Sustain respect and responsibility for collaboration.
6. Sustain inquiry that moves to resolution and shared metacognitive development.
7. Ensure that assessment is aligned with learning outcomes and growth for all students.

The first two principles speak to the social and cognitive challenge of designing a collaborative blended learning experience. The next two principles address the social and cognitive concerns associated with facilitating a Community of Inquiry. The last three principles deal with the social, cognitive, and assessment responsibilities of directing and leading an educational experience to achieve the desired outcomes. These seven principles comprise the first step in providing specific practical guidelines for the design, facilitation, and direction of a collaborative Community of Inquiry in a blended context.

Indigenous Ways of Knowing

As the authors of this book, we are Canadians of European background and thus do not have first-hand experience with Indigenous concepts of learning. Despite this lack of personal experience, we would like to investigate, highlight, and honour Indigenous ways of knowing in light of our seven principles of blended learning. This will take the form throughout the book of providing resources on and references to the work of Indigenous scholars and educators.

To begin, Wilson (2012) indicates that the ability to collaborate is linked to the origin of human intelligence and evolution. Unfortunately, education systems have not always honoured and celebrated students' ability to collaborate. Wolf (2010), in his influential book *Europe and the People without History*, contrasts the Euro-American-centric focus on individual ways of knowing with certain more collaborative Indigenous ways of knowing.

The essence of teaching presence and our seven principles is the reciprocal nature of teaching and learning. This is illustrated in the Maori of New Zealand's concept of *ako*, which means to both teach and learn (Alton-Lee, 2003). *Ako* recognizes the knowledge that both teachers and students bring to learning interactions, and it acknowledges how new knowledge and understanding can grow out of shared learning experiences. Within the Canadian context, Indigenous cultures have embraced collaborative approaches to learning for centuries.

For example, on the eastern coast, the Mi'kmaw Nation of Nova Scotia has developed a "two-eyed seeing" process in order to weave collaboratively Indigenous and Western ways of knowing: that is, "to see from one eye with the strengths of Indigenous ways of knowing, and to see from the other eye with the strengths of Western ways of knowing, and to use both of these eyes together" (Bartlett et al., 2012, p. 335). The Mi'kmaw Nation further indicates that the mind is like a parachute since it works only when it is open to new ideas and ways of knowing.

On the northern coast, the Inuit of Nunavut believe that we learn collaboratively not only from each other but also with and from our natural environment. Based upon this belief, they have developed an educational framework that they refer to as *Inuit Qaujimajatuqangit* (*IQ*). This framework consists of the following eight principles derived from extensive consultations with their Elders (Government of Nunavut, 2007):

- *Inuuqatigiitsiarniq*—respecting others, relationships, and caring for people
- *Tunnganarniq*—fostering good spirit by being open, welcoming, and inclusive
- *Pijitsirniq*—serving and providing for family or community or both
- *Aajiiqatigiinniq*—decision making through discussion and consensus
- *Pilimmaksarniq* or *pijariuqsarniq*—development of skills through practice, effort, and action
- *Piliriqatigiinniq* or *ikajuqtigiinniq*—working together for a common cause
- *Qanuqtuurniq*—being innovative and resourceful

- *Avatittinnik kamatsiarniq*—respect and care for the land, animals, and environment

In addition, on the western coast, the Lil'wat First Nation of Vancouver Island (Sanford et al., 2012) has articulated its own six principles for collaborative learning. They emphasize that learning should benefit the entire community and not just the individual. They also acknowledge that there is a felt energy when a common purpose emerges for a group and that we should seek spaces of stillness and quietness for learning to unfold.

We would like to emphasize that throughout this book we will use resources from and references to Indigenous scholars and educators to investigate, highlight, and honour how Indigenous ways of knowing might align with our seven principles of blended learning.

Conclusion

Our challenge now is to explore how these principles can be used to design, facilitate, and direct blended learning experiences. We will examine systematically strategies and techniques that fuse face-to-face and online learning to create purposeful blended Communities of Inquiry in the support of deep and meaningful approaches to teaching and learning. We need to uncover the strengths and weaknesses of face-to-face and online experiences as we consider each of these principles. We will do so in subsequent chapters that focus on the design, facilitation, direction, and assessment of blended learning experiences.

2 | Design and Organization

Design is the framework that supports learning experiences.
It refers to deliberate choices about what, when, where and
how to teach. Decisions need to be made about the content,
structure, timing, pedagogical strategies, sequence of learning
activities, and the type and frequency of assessment in the
course, as well as the nature of technology used to support
learning.

—(Smart Sparrow, 2022, "Definition"
section)

Considering Design

Our goal in this chapter is to address questions related to the design
of a blended Community of Inquiry that supports interaction and
collaboration in constructing meaning and understanding. More specifically, how do we design an educational experience that combines
the potential for asynchronous online and synchronous face-to-face
discourse in a reflective manner that provides the time to think deeply
and not rush through enormous amounts of content? The challenge
of designing a blended learning experience is balancing the flexibility

and freedom of online learning with the expert guidance found in a purposeful face-to-face learning environment.

The central challenge of a blended design rests on the thoughtful combination of the resources of the internet and the culture of collaborative inquiry in higher education. In addition, Boelens et al. (2017) have identified four key blended learning design challenges based upon a systematic review of the research literature on education: incorporating flexibility, stimulating interaction, facilitating students' learning processes, and fostering an affective learning climate. Thus, design is a planning process that considers the many content and process issues related to the intended learning outcomes. This process inevitably will prove to be more effective and efficient when guided by a coherent framework and shaped by design principles. The first two principles, grounded in the CoI framework, relate to the design and organization of a blended learning course: design for open communication and trust that will create a learning community and design for critical reflection and discourse that will support inquiry.

The first principle of practice is the need to establish a social presence that will support open communication and the development of cohesive group identity. Social presence mediates between teaching and cognitive processes and has been shown to be associated with perceived learning and persistence (Eom & Arbaugh, 2011). The primary goal is to create a climate that encourages and supports open communication through a sense of belonging and trust.

The second principle focuses on the planning of the learning experience itself. The first task is the selection of subject matter, resources, and associated activities. This can be a daunting challenge if we are to encourage deep and meaningful approaches to learning and not overburden students with content and assignments. Please remember the saying "less is more," and focus on conceptual understanding versus content coverage. Gooblar (2021, para. 10) advocates this approach in "Our Slimmed-Down Pandemic Pedagogy": "I would much rather my students read one chapter closely, so that they're able to understand its central concepts and discuss them in class, than skim three chapters and barely remember what they read. I'd rather they put their energies into completing a two-page assignment that engages their abilities in a manageable amount of time than struggle to finish a 10-page paper that brings them more anxiety than knowledge." Designing and organizing a blended course is likely to be more complex and time-consuming than designing a conventional classroom experience. Thinking through the structure, process, and assessment aspects of a blended course raises special challenges. We recommend planning and structuring a blended course by following the phases of the Practical Inquiry model (Garrison et al., 2001). It starts with identifying and defining the challenges associated with a blended course (triggering events). Next we strongly recommend designing your blended learning course in collaboration with a teaching colleague and/or a learning specialist such as an instructional designer. A collaborative approach during the exploration and integration phases can encourage creative ideas and lead to an innovative course design. Finally, the initial design needs to be considered a prototype that will require an iterative process of testing and revision.

Particular macro components to consider in the design of a blended course are

- establishing a curriculum;
- identifying resources;
- defining clear expectations and goals (process and content);
- addressing technological concerns;
- structuring activities (collaborative and individual);
- setting time frames; and
- devising assessment processes and instruments.

Fortunately, there is a variety of high-quality online resources to support the design process of a blended course. Several that we recommend include the University of Calgary's (2022) Blended and Online Learning Resources, the University of Central Florida's (2022) Blended Learning Toolkit, the University of Ottawa's (2022) Blended Toolbox, the University of Wisconsin—Madison's (2022) Blended Learning Toolkit, and Cleveland-Innes and Wilton's (2018) Guide to Blended Learning. In addition, we have created a planning template that teachers can use to design their blended learning courses (see Appendix A or find a digital template that you can print or make a copy at https://tinyurl.com/blendedcoursetemplate).

The key is to begin the design process with the end in mind. What do you want students to take away from your blended course (Wiggins & McTighe, 1998)? How will you constructively align the course learning outcomes with your assessment plans and integration of before, during, and after learning activities (Biggs, 1996)? The following box provides a visual representation of this blended learning design process.

Blended Learning Design Process

Course/Learning Outcomes: What do you want your students to know when they have finished your course (e.g., key learning outcomes: knowledge, skills, and attitudes)?

Assessment Activities: How will you and your students know if they have achieved these learning outcomes (e.g., opportunities for self-, peer-, and instructor assessment)?

Before a Synchronous Session: How will you help students to determine what prior knowledge and experience they have with the assessment activity?

During a Synchronous Session: How will students interact and engage synchronously with the assessment activity?

After a Synchronous Session: What portion of this assessment activity will require "reflective time" for interaction and communication?

> Tools: Which tools can be used to help organize, facilitate, and direct these assessment activities?

Chiang and Wu (2021) have developed a similar framework that they refer to as a three-stage collaborative instructional model (3-CI). This approach integrates pre-class, in-class, and after-class activities and invites students to participate in curriculum implementation and decision making. Their model is an important reminder that designing for collaborative learning in a blended environment is a dynamic and ongoing process. Design issues will continually present themselves as the needs and interests of the Community of Inquiry evolve. Even with the fluid nature of the inquiry, a well-designed course framework will provide greater flexibility at the outset in adjusting to the evolving needs and interests of the community.

In addition, Cleveland-Innes and Dell have developed an open educational resource tool called the Community of Inquiry: Teacher Self-Assessment and Exploration Tool to help in the design, facilitation, and direction of a blended or online course. This tool allows teachers to become practically acquainted with the component parts of the CoI framework while self-assessing indicators of cognitive, social, and teaching presence in their courses. We have created a Google Docs template for this CoI—the Teacher and Self-Assessment Tool—that we invite others to use (see https://tinyurl.com/coiteacher). The tool consists of five columns. The first column is a behavioural indicator related to one of the three CoI presences (cognitive, teaching, and social). The second column allows teachers to rate how the designs of their courses relate to a specific behaviour. The third and fourth columns provide information for teachers to develop a deeper understanding of the learning theory that is the foundation of the CoI framework. The fifth column provides space for teachers to make notes and be explicit about how they are designing and organizing their blended courses for each indicator. A modified version of this tool can be found in Appendix B.

In this chapter, we focus on designing not only for collaborative learning but also for relevance so that students have a sense of curiosity about and connectedness to the learning outcomes for a blended course (Littky & Grabelle, 2004). We describe design strategies and examples that foster the development of cognitive and social presence in a blended course. These activities include the creation of an online needs assessment survey; storytelling; an online discussion forum to share thoughts relevant to intended learning outcomes; the use of digital technologies to clarify course expectations; the use of blogs, concept maps, and a CoI self-assessment tool to help students set their own learning goals and track their progress; and a process for designing effective teamwork.

Online Needs Assessment Survey and Discussion

Students bring prior learning experiences and expectations to all courses in higher education. It is important to gauge those experiences and expectations at the outset of a course. In a blended environment, this can be accomplished by having the students complete an anonymous online needs assessment survey in which they are asked about their expectations of the course. Questions could include the following.

- What are your goals for this course? Bottom line, what do you want to "take away" from your course experience?
- What do you expect will happen during the class sessions? What will the professor do in class, and what will you do?
- What type of work do you expect to do, if any, outside the classroom for this course?
- How do you think your learning in this course will be assessed?
- What type(s) of assistance with your learning do you expect to receive in this course and from whom?

This online survey can be constructed using applications such as Google Forms (Google 2022b), SurveyMonkey (2022), or the survey tool in your institution's learning management system. The key is to share and discuss the survey results with the students during the first synchronous class. The teacher can assign the students to small groups that discuss and synthesize the results of a specific question and then share their key findings with the entire class.

For smaller classes, an alternative to the online survey would be to send out an introductory email with a list of the five questions for students to answer confidentially. You can then digitally compile the results anonymously and review them in the first class so that students can see how they share common hopes for, challenges of, and concerns about the course.

The focus of both approaches is to provide students with an opportunity to co-construct a set of engagement guidelines (rather than rules) that will help to foster open communication and trust that will enable the creation of a learning community. Salhab et al. (2021) have proposed a code of ethics for online learning during a crisis that can be used to guide this process. Through their research, they have developed the following four online ethical principles:

- respect for and protection of digital dignity;
- commitment to the profession;
- commitment to the online education system; and
- teachers' and students' rights and responsibilities within an online learning environment.

Storytelling and the CoI Framework

Everyone has stories to tell, and storytelling can contribute to key social presence elements such as inclusion, connection, and the beginning of a class community (Health Foundation, 2016). Bashovski

(2021) stresses how important storytelling is in the process of building a learning community. Ali (2017) suggests that storytelling can help to create "brave" spaces for inclusion and diversity in a blended course. She suggests that some key guidelines that promote the most productive brave spaces are "controversy with civility," "owning intentions and impacts," "challenge by choice," "respect," and "no attacks" (pp. 3–4). She asserts that these ideas are not hard to implement if they are reinforced through storytelling, the design of the course, the syllabus, and the co-creation of engagement guidelines for the course.

Storytelling has played a central role in passing on certain Indigenous oral histories and teachings. Blackfoot Elder Little Bear (2012) indicates that the power of storytelling is that, each time we tell or hear a story, we learn something new. It is an upward spiral of learning. The Indigenous resource *Sharing through Story* from the Alberta Regional Consortia (2022) also describes how stories can empower students who often feel marginalized in formal educational settings.

During the first week of the course, students can engage in a storytelling exercise in which each reflects on an event that was a compelling learning experience—it might or might not have been related to school. The teacher can create a series of online discussion forums in the course learning management system and then randomly assign four or five students to each forum. First, have the students share their learning experiences in small groups and discuss why they were powerful. Second, debrief as a whole class on what makes the learning experiences powerful and then, using the CoI framework (see Figure 1.1), co-create a set of engagement guidelines for the course.

These discussions should focus on students' roles and responsibilities in a blended learning environment. Encourage students to have conversations about past learning challenges and advice on overcoming them, such as sharing study and time management strategies. It is important to emphasize teach*ing* versus teach*er* presence.

In addition, these initial discussions can help students to share and develop mindfulness practices. Palalas et al. (2020) indicate that students often feel a sense of isolation in blended and online courses and that shared mindfulness practices can help them to overcome this issue. They define "mindfulness" as "the awareness that emerges through paying attention on purpose, in the present moment, and nonjudgmentally to the unfolding of experience moment by moment" (p. 247). They further indicate that this practice can help students to deal with the pressures stemming from the competing responsibilities and emotional demands of being online learners by developing self-regulated learning skills.

Their case study indicates that the key mindfulness-supported habits that positively affect "the forethought, performance, and self-reflection processes were enhanced intrinsic motivation, self-awareness, and a mindful approach to time management" (Palalas et al., 2020, p. 247). However, Austen Kay (2021) reminds us that online mindfulness training is not a panacea for student well-being. He recommends that "it should be seen as one part—albeit a promising one—of a broader strategy for helping students cope with the emotional and psychological consequences of online education in a time of COVID-19" (final para.).

Everyone in the course will be involved in the design, facilitation, and direction of this shared learning experience. The following box provides an example of co-constructed guidelines for online discussion forums in a course.

Ten Engagement Guidelines for Online Discussions

1. Do more than state agreement or disagreement. Justify and support your opinion. The most persuasive opinions are supported by evidence, examples, reasons, and facts. If you disagree with something, then say why.

2. Do the appropriate preparation, such as reading and class activity work, before you join the discussion.

3. Keep your comments brief. A paragraph or two is plenty unless you are posting something that by nature has to be longer—a short story, for example.

4. Check your message before you send it. Pay attention to your spelling and grammar, and be sure that your message makes the points that you want to make in a clear and concise way. Remember that other students and instructors can read your messages.

5. Help to move the discussion along. When contributing to a discussion, read other people's comments first. Introduce new ideas, but also build upon what others have said ("piggyback" on others' ideas).

6. Keep up with the discussion throughout the course. After you have made your contribution on a topic, check back a few times to find out how the discussion is evolving. Does someone's comment make you think twice about your view?

7. Share your experience with other students. You might be able to offer advice to someone who is newer to the course.

8. Respect others' ideas and opinions. Feel free to disagree, but express your disagreement in a respectful manner.

9. Be positive when offering advice. If another student posts something to be edited or asks for your opinion on a piece of writing, then be encouraging with your comments. If you see weaknesses in someone's writing or ideas, then focus on describing the strengths to retain and the opportunities for improvement. Put yourself in the shoes of the other people in the conference discussions.

10. Be gracious when receiving advice. When you post your work, you hope that other people will tell you what you have done well and suggest useful ideas about how to do even better. When others are critical, assume that they are trying to provide critiques, not criticism in the negative sense. Even if they don't seem to be diplomatic, be gracious in your response.

It is also crucial to make the Practical Inquiry model explicit for online discussions and course assignments (see Figure 2.1). In Chapter 4, "Direct Instruction," we describe how students can use the PI model to code and track their own discussion forum posts.

Figure 2.1
Practical Inquiry Model

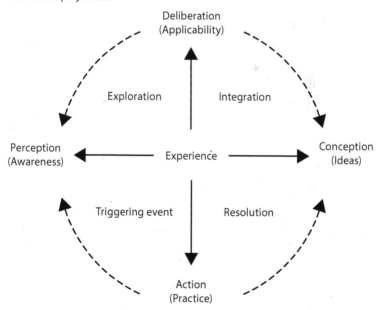

Note. From Garrison et al. (2001).

The key is to make the CoI framework and PI model explicit to students through experiential activities at the outset of a blended course. Explicit introduction of the model allows students to begin to internalize and verbalize the practices associated with our seven principles.

Clarifying Course Learning Outcomes

During the first synchronous session, teachers often review the course outline/syllabus with their students in a lecture format. Unfortunately, this often results in the "in one ear and out the other ear" syndrome. Students do not have the opportunity to discuss and question the expectations of the course. We recommend the following course outline activity. First, randomly place students in teams of approximately four or five students. Each team is responsible for generating at least three questions related to the course outline. These questions can be recorded digitally in applications such as Google Docs (Google 2022a), Padlet (2022), or Google Jamboard (Google 2022c). Depending on the number of students in the class, each team presents its questions, and the teacher responds (see the text box below). For larger classes, teachers are encouraged to aggregate digitally and theme responses to the student questions after the first class and then present and discuss the results in the next class.

Burning Questions from Group One

- For the Twitter account, if we already have one, do you recommend making a new one?
- For our Professional learning plans, are the reflections on all five program competencies completed by our mentor teachers or by us since they are categorized under "Teaching Placement Evaluation"?

- Will we be discussing how to use different software/devices? For example, in one school I know, they use Chromebooks, while another uses Apple devices. I am definitely not confident using any software besides Apple to teach, and I would like to learn more about how to utilize Chromebook to enhance my teaching.

Goal Setting

Once students are clear about the expectations and learning outcomes of a blended course, it is important that they establish their own learning goals and strategies to achieve them. Teachers can design this process by having students use applications such as Google's Blogger (2022) and WordPress (2022) to create reflective learning journals for the course. In their first posts, students can identify their personal learning goals for the course or program (see the text box below).

Example of Personal Learning Goals for a Practicum

Professional responsibilities: Identifies and implements specific changes to practice based upon reflection and feedback from the mentor teacher and faculty supervisor.

Planning for learning: Demonstrates knowledge of learning development and differences and uses this knowledge to plan learning experiences.

Facilitating learning: Uses a variety of teaching strategies to engage learners in rich learning experiences.

Assessment: Uses assessments to identity learners' needs and adjusts instruction, including varied ways of addressing misunderstandings.

Environment: Creates a respectful and an ethical learning community that encourages learners to take risks, build trust, embrace diversity, and increase self-confidence.

Our experience suggests that students have limited prior experience with goal setting and thus require guidance and support in this process. We recommend using the SMART goal approach (Bjerke & Renger, 2017). SMART is an acronym that stands for specific, measurable, achievable, relevant, and timely goal setting.

SMART Goals

Specific: To make a goal specific, you must focus your attention on what you want to achieve.

Measurable: Goals need to be measurable so that you and your students can see when progress is being made.

Achievable: A goal must be achievable. This means that students must feel challenged, but the goal must remain possible.

Relevant: The goal should be personal and relevant to the students: if it matters to them, then they will be more likely to accomplish it.

Timely: The final consideration when setting a goal should be the deadline. Students should consider asking "When will I need to achieve this goal by?"

We recommend that students select critical friend(s) responsible for providing them with constructive feedback and support on the course assignments, such as replying to a blog post about personal learning goals. The critical friend process is a key first step for shared metacognition, which we discuss in more detail in Chapter 3.

An extension to this activity is to have the students generate a set of collaborative goals for the course. Have them create goals in small teams and then digitally compile the results for the entire class. If the list of goals becomes too long, then the students could vote on their top five or 10 using crowdsourcing or voting software applications such as Poll Everywhere (2022) or Mentimeter (Menti, 2022).

Concept Mapping

As we indicated at the beginning of this chapter, "less is more," and the focus of the learning outcomes for a blended course should be on conceptual understanding rather than on content coverage. Thus, concept mapping can be a valuable activity to help students document and track their conceptual growth in a blended course (Figure 2.2). Concept maps are tools for organizing and representing knowledge

Figure 2.2
Conceptual Map of Teaching Competencies

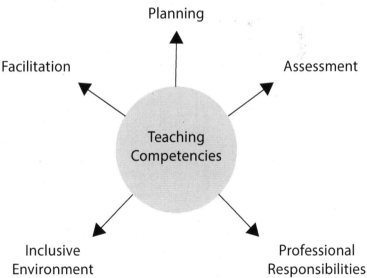

(Novak & Cañas, 2008). A variety of digital technologies can be used for this process. We recommend applications such as Cmap (2022), Coggle (2022), Lucidspark (2022), Miro (2022a), Popplet (2022), or Sketchboard (2022). They are free web-based tools that students can access on a laptop, tablet, or mobile phone.

At the beginning of a blended course, have students use one of these applications to create a digital concept map containing the course's key concepts or learning outcomes. The next step is to ask students to add links to nodes of prior experience with and knowledge of the core concepts. Then throughout the course have designated checkpoints at which students are required to add links to new nodes of knowledge and experience that they are acquiring related to the key concepts. By the end of the course, the students will have created unique visual representations of their acquired knowledge, which they can then articulate further in a reflective writing exercise such as a final course synthesis (Entwistle, 2003).

Students can also use concept maps to create class notes and to design and organize class projects. Brigham Young University (2022) and the University of Waterloo (2022a) provide excellent online resources on other ways that concept maps can be used effectively in blended courses.

Community of Inquiry: Student Self-Assessment Tool

In addition to concept mapping, we have developed a Community of Inquiry: Student Self-Assessment Tool. We have created a Google Docs template for this tool that we invite others to use (see https://tinyurl.com/coistudent). This tool has been designed to help students make practical connections to the CoI framework throughout a course. Similar to the Community of Inquiry: Teacher Self-Assessment and Exploration Tool, the application consists of five columns. The first column is a behavioural indicator related to one of the three CoI presences (cognitive, teaching, and social). The second column allows the students to rate their behaviour at the beginning, midpoint, and end of the course. The third and fourth columns provide information for students to develop a deeper understanding of the learning theory that is the foundation of the CoI framework. The fifth column provides space for students to reflect on and document their development throughout a course. A modified version of this tool can be found in Appendix C.

Designing for Student Group Work

In the next chapter, on facilitation, we provide more details on the formation of student teams, but it is important to have a planning template for this sort of learning activity. We recommend using the IDOARRT design template (Hyper Island, 2022). IDOARRT is the acronym for intention, desired outcome, agenda, rules, roles and responsibilities, and time. It is a simple format to help students engage effectively in teamwork by setting out a clear purpose, a structure, and goals at the beginning of the process.

IDOARRT Meeting Design

Intention: What is the intention or purpose of the teamwork assignment?

Desired outcome(s): Which specific outcomes should be achieved by the end of the assignment?

Agenda: Which activities will the team go through and in what order to move toward the desired outcome(s)?

Roles: Which roles or responsibilities need to be in place for the teamwork to run smoothly? Who is facilitating, and who is participating? Who is documenting, and who is keeping track of the time? What do you expect of each team member?

Rules: Which guidelines will be in place during the meeting? They could relate to established group norms. They could also relate to the use of other apps or practical rules related to learning space. Let the participants add rules to ensure that they have ownership of them.

Time: What are the time frame and milestones for the assignment?

The results of this design process can be recorded digitally in Google Docs (Google, 2022a) or an online template from the collaborative whiteboard application Miro (2022b). In addition, Miro (2022c) has developed a guide to help students learn to collaborate in blended or hybrid environments. This handbook consists of chapters on engagement and inclusivity, continuous collaboration, alignment, and tying it all together.

Conclusion

For a blended course, it is important to design and scaffold learning activities that support shared thinking and learning (shared metacognition) with an ethic of care for inclusivity (socio-emotional presence). It is important to keep in mind that creating a learning community takes time, so repetition and patience are important. To keep learners engaged and progressing toward intended learning outcomes necessitates leadership, specifically in facilitation. In the next chapter, we explore facilitation strategies and activities for creating and sustaining a community of inquiry in a blended course.

3 | Facilitation

If you teach a person what to learn, you are preparing that
person for the past. If you teach the person how to learn, you
are preparing them for the future.

—(Houle, 1954, p. 372)

Facilitation of blended learning refers to arranging and supporting
student-learning activities in both online and face-to-face classrooms.
According to Bonk et al., (2004, p. 17), "blended learning is typically
more complicated and multifaceted than either fully online or face-to-
face learning. . . . [T]eachers must know when to shift gears or add new
tasks or resources and when to let students wander off and explore
their own interests." Facilitation is the central activity in an educational
Community of Inquiry for developing worthwhile learning experiences as well as awareness and strategies (shared metacognition) through
sustained reflection and discourse among students and the teacher.
Facilitative actions, "on the part of both the students and the teacher,
create the climate, support discourse, and monitor learning. In the act
of facilitation, students connect with each other, engage with the content, are cognitively present as intellectual agents, and carry out all

actions central to the development and maintenance of the learning community" (Vaughan et al., 2013, p. 46).

The blending of online and face-to-face interactions results in a new learning environment that necessitates significant role adjustments for teachers and students (Cleveland-Innes et al., 2007). This transition from a teacher-centred to a learning-centred environment can be a challenge since many of us in higher education are conditioned to "teach how we were taught," focusing on content delivery rather than the facilitation of learning. As a result, there is a need to understand the concept of teaching presence for deep and meaningful learning outcomes since the focus is now on the learning process and conceptual understanding rather than content coverage. The CoI principles of facilitation—establishing community and cohesion and inquiry dynamics (purposeful inquiry) for social and cognitive presence in a blended environment—are part of this required change.

The third principle is associated with social presence and focused on group identity and cohesion through open communication (Garrison, 2016). For students to be present socially, they must have the opportunity to interact. A Community of Inquiry emerges and maintains itself through the purposeful engagement, interaction, and relationships among members of the group. The teacher begins this process by encouraging, modelling, and supporting activities that allow each member of the group to become familiar with and possibly find a link to other members of the group. The nature and importance of these links become measures of the amount of cohesion found within each group and determine whether the group will or will not become a community. The more developmental and meaningful the engagement and interaction, the stronger the links, the greater the cohesion, and the more likely that deep and meaningful learning will occur. In a blended environment, this requires encouraging and modelling such activity both face-to-face and online.

The fourth principle is related to cognitive presence and reflects the facilitation of the process of inquiry. The Practical Inquiry process (Garrison et al., 2001) goes to the heart of cognitive presence and requires increasing amounts of cognitive effort and complexity. This process of changing complexity must be facilitated through appropriate discourse from a triggering event, exploration, integration to resolution, or application. Facilitation is necessary to set in motion and guide the dynamics of inquiry. In a blended environment, integrated face-to-face and online learning opportunities can allow for increased interaction, timely reflection, and continuous debate, all of which help to support the process of inquiry.

In essence, the teacher is responsible for modelling the development of shared metacognition in a course by helping to create and sustain constructive learning relationships (Littky & Grabelle, 2004). Creating a sense of community and collaboration is key to helping students develop their capacity (awareness and proficiency) for shared metacognition. Unfortunately, studies indicate that many students in higher education have little formal experience working collaboratively (Chang & Brickman, 2018). This chapter provides activities and resources for helping students to learn how to work successfully in groups.

Group Development

As we have indicated, many students in higher education have limited experience and guidance with how to work collaboratively. From our perspective, it is important to provide students with a rationale for group work (why bother?) as well as first-hand experience with a group development process. In terms of a rationale, we recommend having students read an article such as Theodora's (2019) "Five Reasons Why You Should Love Group Work." Then place students in groups and have them debrief about the article and identify

- the learning opportunities that group work provides;
- the challenges of group work; and
- recommendations on how they would like to work as a group.

With regard to providing students with first-hand experience, we recommend the design and facilitation of collaborative activities that utilize Tuckman's (1965) five stages of group development (see Figure 3.1). The model has withstood the test of time and consists of forming, storming, norming, performing, and re-forming/transforming phases.

Ideally, a low-stakes activity should be designed and facilitated at the beginning of the semester so that students can obtain a

Figure 3.1

Developmental Sequence in Small Groups

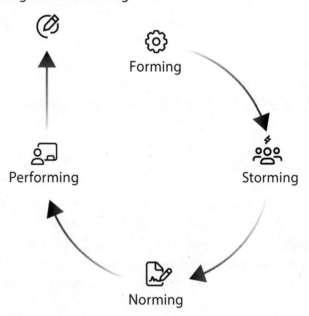

Re-forming or Transforming

Forming

Storming

Norming

Performing

Note. Adapted from Tuckman (1965).

first-attempt-in-learning experience. In the case of an educational technology course, this could involve students working together on a case study to develop a solution to a school-related problem or issue (Schoology Exchange, 2017). The key is for the students to create a sense of shared metacognition through this group development process (see Figure 1.3). Shared metacognition is a process by which students take responsibility for and control of the processes of inquiry and learning. It represents awareness as well as personal and shared regulation of the learning process.

This can be accomplished by having students document collaboratively their metacognitive awareness of and strategies used for each of the five stages of Tuckman's (1965) model. Students can then apply this new knowledge to monitor and manage their shared metacognition in the subsequent collaborative activities and projects of a blended course.

Medicine Wheel

The COVID-19 pandemic demonstrated the need to pay greater attention to students' social-emotional well-being, especially in relation to group work, which can cause additional stress and conflict. Some teachers have begun to introduce the Indigenous Medicine Wheel framework in their blended and online courses in order to emphasize multicultural ways of knowing and being resilient.

The Medicine Wheel is a circle that consists of four quadrants. There are different ways that Indigenous Elders interpret these quadrants, such as the four directions, the four teachings, the four winds, and other relationships that can be expressed in sets of four (Bell, 2014). Often these four quadrants refer to the importance of balancing one's spiritual, physical, emotional, and mental capacities. The Anishinaabe have used the Medicine Wheel to develop a framework for Indigenous education that they call the Gift of Four Directions, in some respects very similar to Garrison et al.'s (2000) Practical Inquiry model (see Figure 3.2).

In the east quadrant, where the sun rises, the gift of vision is found, and one is able to see or identify the triggering event. In the south quadrant, one spends time relating to the vision, the exploration phase. In the west, one uses the gift of reason to figure it out, the integration phase. And in the north, one uses the gift of movement to do or actualize the vision, the application and resolution phase.

Cajete (1994, p. 42) emphasizes that learning and change will not "come into existence in a linear way, as the result of a single-minded drive, but in a cyclic, circular, collaborative way, working in all dimensions of a culture, moving from one position to another, not in reaction but in interaction with other forces." He adds that moving from linear

Figure 3.2
Gift of Four Directions

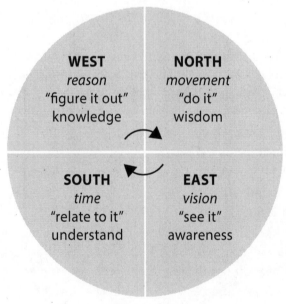

Note. From Bell (2014).

models to the interconnectedness of the circle can guide the development of pedagogy and vision for the future.

Absolon (2019, p. 36) states that "the teaching and healing process is evolutionary and cyclical in nature, as is the continuum of medicine wheels. It begins with a desire to understand and identify with the balance, wholeness and interconnectedness expressed in the medicine wheel."

Structured Reading Groups

One particularly effective collaborative activity in a blended course is the use of structured reading groups (Parrott & Cherry, 2011). Two common challenges in higher education are getting students to complete course readings and having them engage in deep rather than superficial (scanning) reading. Structured reading groups can facilitate both deep reading and active discussion of course material. Early in the semester, students are assigned to small groups of six with a set of rotating group roles: discussion leader, passage master, creative connector, devil's advocate, reporter, and choice.

In a blended course, the process begins with a pre-class activity. The entire class is provided with a reading related to key course concepts, and each student is assigned a particular role in the small group (see the text box below for a breakdown of these roles). Students are then responsible for completing the reading and posting a contribution to a discussion forum related to their assigned roles.

Structured Reading Group Roles

Discussion leader. Your job is to review the readings and come up with two to three questions for the group. The questions need to capture the main points or takeaways. You will also guide the online and face-to-face discussions, which means keeping track of time and asking others to share their questions and insights from their own preparations. You will encourage critical discussion, respectful disagreement, and debate but work to keep the discussion on track. Probe with an open question such as "Can you tell us more?" or "Can you give a specific example?" or "Why?"

Passage master. Your job is to review the assigned reading and highlight two critical passages. These passages have caught your attention for some reason, such as they eloquently capture the main points, or they are confusing and/or contradictory. Although your preparation should include the page numbers and/or locations of the passages, it must also include brief summaries of the passages and more detailed explanations of why you wish to draw the group's attention to the passages.

Creative connector. As the name implies, you connect the readings to other ideas. These ideas can be social, political, or cultural. In MacPherson and Cherry's (2011, p. 357) words, "this may include making connections to other reading assignments or artifacts in popular culture (advertisements, YouTube clips, cartoons, discussions of movies, etc.)." Some examples are a particular episode of *The Big Bang Theory*, a popular internet meme, a magazine ad, a TED talk, a personal photograph, a famous work of art, a familiar building, and a Disney character. It can also be a personal connection: something that happened to you as a child, a favourite saying of an elderly uncle, et cetera. Post your idea to the discussion forum. You need to include enough details for your group to understand the connections that you are making.

Devil's advocate. In this role, you act as a critic. Develop a list of questions that challenge or poke holes in the main theories, ideas, and examples presented in the reading. Is there another side to the story? Are competing interests presented fairly? Which questions are left unanswered? What are some differing ideas or competing theories? Whose voices or experiences are not included? How does this stack up with historical practice? What are the pros and cons of the arguments presented? This role gives students explicit permission to disagree with the course material and to develop arguments contrary to popular opinion. Use one or two of these questions to guide your contribution.

Reporter. In this role, you have a laptop and take notes on the group discussion in a collaborative application such as Google Docs (Google, 2022a). This online and face-to-face discussion synthesis includes both points of general agreement and especially points of contention or disagreement. Highlight critical elements examined and sum up main points discussed. Find internet links for connections brought up as part of the discussion and include them in the discussion summary. Note points of confusion, areas for future study, or particular areas that students found interesting. You might also be asked to report back verbally to the entire class.

Choice. The sixth student can choose among devil's advocate, creative connector, and passage master. This means that there will be more than one person in each group sharing one of those roles.

During class, students are given approximately 20 minutes to meet in their structured reading groups. They have time to discuss, debrief, and synthesize further the assigned reading. We strongly encourage the reporters to create their discussion summaries in a collaborative application such as Google Docs (Google, 2022a) so that these summaries can be linked and accessed by other students in the course learning management system. If time permits, we also recommend selecting one group for each class to provide an oral report of their discussion summary. It is important that all students are given an opportunity to take on each role in a structured reading group, and the following grid provides an example of a schedule for a blended course.

Structured Reading Group Schedule for a Blended Course

Date/ Summary	Member 1	Member 2	Member 3	Member 4	Member 5	Member 6
Week 1	Discussion director	Passage master	Creative connector	Devil's advocate	Reporter	Choice
Week 2	Choice	Discussion director	Passage master	Creative connector	Devil's advocate	Reporter
Week 3	Post examples of your Universal Design for Learning (UDL) guideline and how it might be used in classrooms.					
Week 4	Reporter	Choice	Discussion director	Passage master	Creative connector	Devil's advocate
Week 5	Respond to questions corresponding to your group number on the discussion board.					
Week 6	Respond to questions corresponding to your group number on the discussion board.					
Week 7	Devil's advocate	Reporter	Choice	Discussion director	Passage master	Creative connector
Week 8	Creative connector	Devil's advocate	Reporter	Choice	Discussion director	Passage master
Week 9	Passage master	Creative connector	Devil's advocate	Reporter	Choice	Discussion director

In the previous chapter, on design, we emphasized the importance of co-creating a set of engagement guidelines and provided an example for online discussions. For a blended course, we also recommend developing a set of guidelines for face-to-face discussions. The following text box highlights some suggestions.

Seven Suggested Guidelines for Face-to-Face Discussions

1. You owe it to the group members to come prepared for critical discussion. And you owe it to yourself to take advantage of the opportunity to learn from the ideas of your peers.

2. Disagreement is encouraged but must be respectful at all times.

3. You are responsible for the energy and tone that you bring to the space through your participation.

4. Rather than jump in with quick disagreement, listen first to the other side of an argument, and try to understand the rationale behind the differing viewpoint.

5. Come prepared with evidence and examples to back up your opinions and contentions.

6. As opposed to asking questions with fixed "yes" or "no" answers, ask about the "why" or "how." Listen to the rationales offered.

7. Agreed upon group conclusions are not required; many areas are grey.

World Café Conversations

Another method of structuring blended discussions is engaging in World Café Conversations (2022). Brown and Isaacs (2005) developed this conversational framework. World Café is a discussion protocol that fosters diverse conversations on important topics. Typically, it is held as three rounds of discussion on questions of increasing complexity. Table groups of four or five participants spend time on each question and "harvest" their thinking via a summary statement identifying the pattern or theme that emerged from the conversation. Between each round, groups are "shuffled" so that participants can connect with different people who bring a range of ideas and perspectives.

In a face-to-face environment, the World Café method (Primera, 2019) consists of the following five components.

World Café Method

1. *Setting.* Set up are round tables with flip chart paper and markers or a laptop and the use of a collaborative writing application such as Google Docs.

2. *Welcome and introduction.* The key is to make the students of the World Café feel welcome and safe with an introduction and to set the context of your class World Café.

3. *Small group rounds.* The process starts with the first of three 20-minute rounds of conversation in the small groups seated around a table. At the end of the 20 minutes, each member of the group moves to a different table. They might or might not choose to leave one person as the "table host" who welcomes the next group and briefly fills them in on what happened in the previous round.

4. *Questions.* Questions (triggering events) are one of the most important aspects of the World Café. Asking a powerful question that starts the process is vital, so take your time with it.

5. *Harvest.* After the three rounds of conversation are done, the groups are invited to share their insights and reflect on the whole process. They can use the flip chart paper or a digital method to report the key findings from their conversations.

One of the recommendations in the *EDUCAUSE Horizon Report* (Pelletier et al., 2021) is that higher education classrooms need to be reconfigured to support blended learning approaches that utilize large-scale collaborative activities such as the World Café approach.

Recently, Hite (2020) has adapted the World Café method for online discussion forums. He suggests that the COVID-19 pandemic has led to Zoom fatigue and Webex weariness and that it is important to utilize strategies to reduce that tiredness and provide meaningful online experiences. He emphasizes the importance of first establishing a purpose for the session; students must always be clear why they are spending time in conversation together. After the purpose has been established, Hite recommends developing collaboratively a set of questions to guide each of the three rounds. Similar to the face-to-face format, the questions must be important and worth exploring. He recommends questions that increase gradually in complexity, beginning with a broader and less personal question for the first round, focusing on more personal experiences in the second round, and ultimately homing in on what the conversation might inspire in the third round.

Students should also be provided with instructions on how to harvest the thinking between each round so that they can capture patterns and themes that emerge during each conversation. Hite (2020) indicates that the word *harvest* is both a verb and a noun, and both are required in order to capture the essence of the conversation. The following instructions illustrate a process for harvesting a conversation.

Instructions for Harvesting a World Café Discussion

Group discussion: Which patterns emerged during our conversation?

Group reflection: How best might we share what we noticed?

Sharing: Prepare a summative statement that captures the pattern or theme to be shared with a larger group or the entire class.

Conducting a virtual World Café can be facilitated by using web-conferencing applications such as Google Meet (Google, 2022d), MS Teams (2022), and Zoom (2022). These applications can be used to move students easily into breakout rooms for the conversational rounds. Students in each room are asked to nominate a conversation host responsible for guiding the discussion and creating a summary statement to capture key patterns and themes. The broadcast feature in web conferencing applications allows the teacher to post the question and provide time checks to keep the groups on track.

When a conversational round is completed, the groups return to the main room, and each host is asked to type the summary into the chat window to share it with the entire class. Doing so allows everyone to notice and share commonalities or differences among the breakout conversations. When it is time for the next round, students are shuffled randomly into new conversation groups, and the host facilitation pattern is repeated.

Hite (2020) reports that web-conferencing applications make it easy and efficient to get students into conversation groups because no one has to move physically to a table. Another benefit is that the harvest from each round is typed into the chat window, so immediately everyone has a digital record of each group's thinking.

Critical Friends

Besides group work, the use of critical friends has been introduced in many institutions of higher education that see themselves as learning organizations and know that learning requires honest and regular feedback (Senge, 1990). A critical friend provides such feedback. As the name suggests, a critical friend is a trusted person who asks provocative questions, provides data to be examined through another lens, and offers critiques of a person's work as a friend (Lambrev & Cruz, 2021). A critical friend takes the time to understand fully the context of the work presented and the outcomes toward which the person or group is working. The friend is an advocate for the success of that work (Costa & Kallick, 1993).

Since the concept of critique often carries negative connotations, a critical friendship requires trust and a formal process. Many people equate critique with judgment, and when someone offers criticism they brace themselves for negative comments. We often forget that Bloom et al. (1956) refer to critique as a part of evaluation, one of the highest orders of thinking in their original taxonomy.

There has been a great deal of discussion about the formation of critical friends (Bambino, 2002). The two main options are having students select their own friends and having the teacher assign them. The issue with students who select their own friends is that they are often reluctant to provide honest and meaningful feedback since they might not want to upset their friends.

Regardless of how critical friends are selected, the process must begin by building trust (social presence). The critical friends need to agree that they will

- be clear about the nature of the relationship and not use it for assessment or judgment;
- listen well by clarifying ideas, encouraging specificity, and taking time to understand fully what is being presented;
- offer value judgments only upon request from the learner;
- respond to the learner's work with integrity; and
- be an advocate for the success of the work.

Once this sense of trust has been established, the critical friends meet in a conference. The time allowed for this conference is flexible, but we have found it useful to limit the conference to 20 minutes. Once critical friends are accustomed to the structure, the time can be shortened. We recommend the following guidelines for facilitating the conference.

Guidelines for Facilitating a Critical Friend Conference Session

1. The student describes the assignment and requests feedback. For example, a student might describe a writing assignment or project.

2. The critical friend asks questions in order to understand the assignment described and to clarify the context of the assignment. For example, the friend might ask the student "What do you hope other people will learn from your project?"

3. The student sets desired outcomes for this conference. This allows the student to be in control of the feedback.

4. The critical friend provides feedback on what seems to be significant about the assignment. This feedback provides more than cursory praise; it also provides a lens through which to elevate the work. For example, the student's critical friend might say "I think your project will be significant because you are trying to bring a new insight into the way people have understood the changing role of women in Canada."

5. The critical friend raises questions and critiques the work, nudging the student to see the assignment from different perspectives. Typical queries might be "When you do this project, how will you help others to follow your presentation?"

6. Both participants reflect and write. The student writes notes on the conference, an opportunity to think about points and suggestions raised. For example, the student might reflect on questions such as "Will changes make this work better or worse?" and "What have I learned from this refocusing process?" The critical friend writes to the student with suggestions or advice appropriate to the desired outcome. This part of the

process is different from typical feedback situations in that the student does not have to respond or make any decision on the basis of the feedback. Instead, the student reflects on the feedback without needing to defend the work to the critical friend.

Vaughan and Lee Wah (2020) investigated the use of critical friends in a third-year blended educational technology course. The students involved in this study identified the following benefits of the critical friend process.

- Improving the quality of my work. He was also able to give me some constructive feedback that always ended up benefiting my assignment (Student 17).
- New perspectives and ideas. They were very beneficial because it helped me to see concepts and topics from different perspectives, and it challenged my opinions (Student 9).
- Friendship, collaboration, and support. I was able to form more connections this semester. I talked to people I have not talked to before and worked with people I have not worked with before (Student 10).
- Stay focused, keep on track and motivated. Having someone as a reminder to help keep one another on task and motivated (Student 6).
- Peer teaching and learning opportunities (teaching presence). Was able to bounce ideas off another individual and practise giving constructive feedback (Student 2).

Conversely, the same group of students identified the following challenges of the critical friend process.

- Providing feedback online is challenging. It was hard meeting with my constructive friend online. I think in person would be better (Student 1).

- Communication and scheduling challenges. Sometimes we had conflicting ideas or schedules, which made it hard to work together or get some of the responses back for the blog (Student 2).
- Not being able to be a reliable constructive friend. I was behind this semester, so I was not always able to give my friend the feedback that was needed (Student 1).
- Different perspectives. It was challenging to work with other people simply because of their very different perspectives (Student 3).
- Pathological politeness. Giving feedback can sometimes feel challenging because you don't want to hurt someone's feelings. Although we know that it's coming from a loving place, it can be challenging (Student 3).

In terms of recommendations for improving the critical friend process, the students provided the following suggestions.

- Mixing up the constructive friend pairings throughout the semester. I didn't like the idea of working with *only one person* for every single meeting (constructive friend). This should have been mixed up. I only received one person's perspective for the entire semester. It would have been way more beneficial to mix it up and have others to comment on my blog post (Student 22).
- Have the teacher select the constructive friends. Random picking of friends by the teacher was great because I got to work with someone I didn't know (Student 32).
- Peer review accountability process. Having some sort of peer assessment process for the accountability and quality of feedback from our constructive friend (Student 8).

Student-Moderated Discussions

Finally, an effective way for students to appreciate metacognitive awareness and co-regulation of the learning experience is to have the students in a blended course moderate online and face-to-face discussions. Doing so provides students with the opportunity to learn experientially the art of facilitating discussions in terms of knowing when to intervene, when to move the discussion along, and when to summarize key points.

It has been demonstrated that peer facilitation can increase engagement and cognitive presence (deNoyelles et al., 2014). Student moderators are less intimidating and therefore have the ability to engage and draw in more participants to the discussion. Rourke and Anderson (2002) indicate that higher-order thinking can be achieved when discussions are facilitated by peers. In addition, Dennen (2005) reports that the level of dialogue is higher when the teacher is actively involved but not dominating the discussion.

We recommend that the teacher moderate the first online and face-to-face discussions in a blended course. That way the teacher can demonstrate, model, and debrief the expected requirements for a discussion moderator. In terms of guidelines, Wise (2020) has developed a set of roles for students to reflect on as they moderate an online discussion forum. These roles could also be adapted for face-to-face discussions in a blended course.

Student Moderation Roles for Online Discussions

Role 1: Starter

Goal
Kick the discussion off right by sharing ideas, asking questions, and raising what you see as the most important issues to discuss.

- What are the most important ideas in the course material? Have new ideas been introduced?

- How do the ideas in the material fit together? Do they support each other? Or do they offer different points of view?

- Which concepts are difficult? Which ideas do you want to understand better?

Ways to Take Action

- Be ready to contribute to the discussion as soon as it opens.

- Focus on the course material, but make your posts broad enough that your peers can add their own perspectives.

- Provide new ideas if a discussion seems to have stalled.

Role 2: Motivator/Responder

Goal

Make the discussion a place in which everyone feels comfortable and encouraged to participate.

Questions to Ask Yourself

- Is everyone contributing? Are a few people dominating the conversation?

- Are everyone's ideas being acknowledged and addressed?

Ways to Take Action

- If someone's posts aren't getting responses, then try to make a point of replying to them.

- If someone's ideas aren't clear, then try asking for clarification or reflecting on what you think the person said (e.g., "Are you saying that . . . ?"). If you see examples of people dominating the discussion or shutting others down, then let your instructor know.

Role 3: Elaborator/Questioner

Goal

Ask your peers to go deeper, elaborate an issue, or defend their ideas. Entertain different arguments and ask for evidence. Consider counterarguments.

Questions to Ask Yourself

- Is the argument in a post well reasoned? Does it have evidence to support claims, or is it based primarily upon an opinion? Does it draw from course readings, research, or theory?

- Which objections can be made to the argument? What about possible counterarguments to this position?

- Does the group seem to be in complete agreement at the outset without fully considering alternatives?

Ways to Take Action

- Be a questioner. Ask "Why do you think X?" or "What implications does your point have for Y?"

- Be an elaborator. Take others' ideas further by building upon them or their implications.

- Be a devil's advocate. Take a contrary position to a classmate's idea and make a reasonable defence of it as a logical position to take (and be respectful while doing so).

- Be an angel's advocate. Provide support for an idea being challenged.

Role 4: Traffic Director

Goal

Keep the discussion moving in a positive direction. Get the discussion back on track if it stalls.

Questions to Ask Yourself

- Are we questioning our ideas? Are we building upon each other's contributions? Are we generating new ideas? Are we critiquing and comparing existing ones? Are we working toward a collective synthesis? (If your group isn't asking any of these questions, then you might be stalled or off track.)

- Were enough different ideas generated initially?

- Is our discussion addressing the questions that we asked ourselves at the beginning? What has been lost inadvertently along the way?

Ways to Take Action

- If the discussion seems to be off track or ideas have been dropped, then make a post bringing up these ideas or pointing out where you think the discussion needs to go.

- If the discussion has stalled, then try introducing some new ideas to the conversation or raise some of the initial questions again if they haven't been answered.

- Often a stalled discussion is a sign that it's time to summarize what's already been discussed. Seeing the big picture can help you to find new ways to move forward.

Role 5: Synthesizer

Goal

Make connections among posts, pull comments together, summarize key ideas, and point out overlapping thoughts, problematic issues, and unresolved questions. Push the conversation forward (maybe in new directions).

Questions to Ask Yourself

- Given everyone's initial posts and any discussion that has resulted, where are we at in terms of answering the questions that we posed (or others that have arisen)?
- What do we as a group agree on? What do we disagree on?
- What have we still not discussed/resolved?
- What other important ideas/themes have arisen during the discussion?
- What have we not considered yet?

Ways to Take Action

- Create a post about halfway through your discussion that summarizes where things stand.
- Identify where you think the conversation needs to go next.
- You might want to highlight individual contributions or focus on group ideas; this will depend on the discussion. If you are naming individuals, then think about how you are portraying them and their ideas, and try not to focus on any one person's ideas too much.

Conclusion

In this chapter, we have demonstrated that integrating online and face-to-face engagement results in a blended learning environment that necessitates significant role adjustments for teachers in higher education. Educators must become facilitators of learning rather than delivery vehicles of content. They must become more than a "guide on the side or sage on the stage." Facilitators must model the "ways of thinking in their disciplinary or professional practice" (Vaughan et al., 2013, p. 46). Of all the aspects of the CoI framework, the activities of facilitation are the most critical. Facilitation monitors and manages the overlaps (setting climate, supporting discourse, and regulating learning) between the presences and is at the core of the dynamics of a Community of Inquiry (see Figure 1.1).

Facilitation is most critical in the earliest stages of interaction, whereas direct instruction becomes more important as the complexity and cognitive load of a task or an assignment increase. Our experience suggests that facilitation is necessary to set in motion the dynamics of inquiry, but direct instruction is required when techniques of facilitation no longer move the process of inquiry to the integration and resolution/application phases. Our focus in the next chapter is on strategies of direct instruction that "nudge" students further along in their process of inquiry and help to improve their ability to monitor and manage shared metacognition.

4 | Direct Instruction

*Teaching presence is not possible without the expertise of a
pedagogically experienced and knowledgeable teacher who
can identify worthwhile content, organize learning activities,
guide the discourse, offer additional sources of information,
diagnose misconceptions, and provide conceptual order when
required. These are direct and proactive interventions that
support an effective and efficient learning experience.*

—(Garrison, 2017, p. 76)

Direct instruction is not about lecturing; rather, it is about scholarly
and pedagogical leadership. It is an essential ingredient of any formal
educational experience in order to help students learn how to take
responsibility collaboratively to monitor and manage their learning
(shared metacognition). It has been shown that students expect structure and leadership in higher education courses, and the roles and
responsibilities of direct instruction should be shared by all members
of a Community of Inquiry (Garrison & Cleveland-Innes, 2005). Individual and collaborative metacognition serves to guide the process of
inquiry and to encourage timely progression toward learning goals.
Direct instruction is about ensuring that students achieve the intended

learning outcomes of a course or program, and it is related specifically to the fifth principle, sustain respect and responsibility for collaboration, and the sixth principle, sustain inquiry that moves to resolution and shared metacognitive development.

The fifth principle is associated with social presence responsibilities. This principle focuses on sustaining a supportive environment and addressing issues that can undermine the group's trust and sense of belonging. Recall that social presence is concerned with open communication, group cohesion, and interpersonal relationships. Maintaining an open and cohesive Community of Inquiry requires a sensitive and sustained focus on the intended learning outcomes (identification with the purpose of the course). Sustaining the climate, being committed to the purposeful collaborative process, and developing interpersonal relationships are the essence of this principle. During the process of facilitation, the initial challenge is to establish these properties of a Community of Inquiry. Once established, the ongoing challenge is to ensure that they are sustained and to address issues that can undermine the climate that mediates academic discourse.

The sixth principle addresses issues of cognitive presence. This concerns scholarly leadership and is associated with critical discourse, reflection, and progression through the phases of Practical Inquiry. Direct instruction is tasked specifically with ensuring systematic and disciplined inquiry. Sustaining purposeful inquiry includes several overlapping responsibilities. They include providing students with ongoing feedback and academic direction. The overriding responsibility of direct instruction is to ensure that students move through the phases of inquiry and do so in a timely manner. This was one of the challenges revealed in the early research on the CoI framework (Garrison, 2017). In addition to task design deficiencies, it was found that direct instruction was lacking in terms of moving to the resolution phase. Ensuring progression to that phase in the context of collaborative inquiry requires that students maintain a focus on the task, which requires resolution, and that issues are resolved quickly.

The focus of direct instruction is also on rigour (Littky & Grabelle, 2004). A higher education course should involve students in completing a challenging problem, task, or assignment that forces them to confront different perspectives and new ways of thinking. This process involves the teacher in "nudging" the students forward in their academic studies (Thaler & Sunstein, 2008). For example, students are often content to share and discuss ideas with each other but require encouragement to integrate and apply those ideas in course assignments and everyday life.

We have indicated in previous chapters that teaching presence in a blended Community of Inquiry is developmental and collaborative. As a semester or unit of academic studies progresses, it is important that students share and assume more of the responsibilities for its design, facilitation, and direction. Unfortunately, as we have seen in previous chapters, students often lack the experience and self-confidence to take on these roles. For example, in a recent study by Vaughan and Lee Wah (2020), students in an educational technology course reported finding it difficult to challenge their peers' strategies and perspectives (see Figures 4.1 and 4.2).

The Likert-type scale for this figure demonstrates that students had a range of comfort levels with challenging their peers. With regard to strategies related to direct instruction, students commented specifically on work ethic and quality of work. Several of the students quoted the Pareto principle (Asad, 2013) in which 20% of the group does 80% of the work: "Usually one or two people ended up doing the work while other group members didn't do anything" (Student blog 11). In terms of quality, one participant commented that "being able to trust others and their level of work is something I found difficult. I always want to try to strive for perfection (even when unattainable), so if I

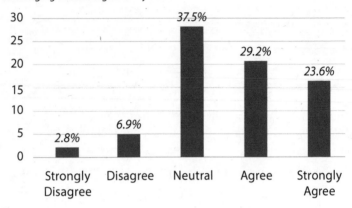

Figure 4.1

Challenging the Strategies of My Peers

feel others are not as invested or do not put in as much work/effort, it makes me upset" (Student blog 52).

The students in Vaughan and Lee Wah's (2020) study also commented on the challenge of negotiating different perspectives during group work (see Figure 4.2). For example, one participant stated that "sometimes it can be difficult to cooperate with others that have different ideas and values. However, this is still a valuable experience" (Student blog 13). Another student explained how overcoming this type of challenge can be an important learning experience: "I had some group members that were quick to shut down others' ideas without backing up why. This was frustrating and at times hard to deal with, but it taught me to speak up and skills to positively work through an uncomfortable situation" (Student blog 33).

Garrison (2017, p. 53) has also documented how students often are unwilling to disagree with or challenge each other in a higher education course, especially in online discussion forums, since they do not want to offend or hurt anyone's feelings, a sense of "pathological politeness." In this chapter, then, we focus on providing guidelines, examples, activities, and resources that teachers can use to help students gain

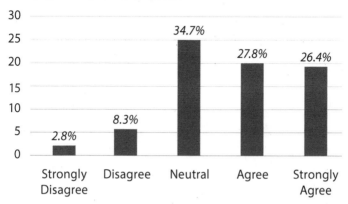

Figure 4.2

Challenging the Perspectives of My Peers

experience and self-confidence with direct instruction in a blended Community of Inquiry.

Cyclical Nature of Inquiry

"We teach how we were taught" is a common saying, and many of us in higher education focus on an individualistic, linear approach to learning and therefore find it challenging to adapt to a cyclical and iterative approach to inquiry. In the previous chapter, "Facilitation," we discussed how Garrison et al.'s (2000) Practical Inquiry model aligned with the Anishinaabe Medicine Wheel framework for education (Bell, 2014). Both models consist of four interconnected quadrants that students move through in a cyclical nature.

In the CoI framework (Garrison, 2017), the PI model is interconnected with social and teaching presence. The Medicine Wheel involves balancing one's spiritual, physical, emotional, and mental capacities (Toulouse, 2016). Shanker (2014, p. 1) states that, "instead of seeing reason and emotion as belonging to separate and independent faculties (the former controlling the latter), they [a multitude of researchers] argue that social, emotional and cognitive processes are all bound together in a seamless web." This recognition of interconnectedness as a primary concept in learning and emotional development is central to some Indigenous views of education (Carriere, 2010; Iseke, 2010). The key for us as educators is to demonstrate explicitly to our students the cyclical and interconnected nature of inquiry.

Inquiry-Based Assignment Guidelines

It is important for teachers to model and provide guidelines for the process of inquiry. In this regard, we should remember that inquiry-based learning is not a specific technique but a process that requires metacognitive awareness to enhance intellectual engagement and deep understanding (Pedaste et al., 2015). An inquiry-based approach to learning encourages students to

- develop their questioning, research, and communication skills;
- collaborate outside the classroom;
- solve problems, create solutions, and tackle real-life questions and issues; and
- participate in the creation and amelioration of ideas and knowledge.

We recommend the use of Garrison et al.'s (2001) PI model to direct the process of inquiry. Recall that this model is based upon the cognitive presence element of the CoI framework (Garrison, 2017) and involves four phases of inquiry: triggering event, exploration, integration, and resolution.

In online discussion assignments, students can use the PI model to self-code their forum posts in order to help them develop their metacognitive awareness and strategies related to direct instruction. For example, they can label their posts as a triggering event, an exploration, an integration, or a resolution comment.

It is important to remember that this is a dynamic model that moves iteratively between reflection (deliberation) and discourse (action) and does not necessarily occur in a linear format. However, for metacognitive awareness and inquiry-based assignments, the four phases can be presented to students in the following format.

1. *Triggering event*: Clarify and define the questions for inquiry.
2. *Exploration*: Explore different perspectives and probe various situations and contexts.
3. *Integration*: Conduct analyses and provide descriptions.
4. *Resolution/application*: Communicate findings, in writing or verbally, using various forms of digital technologies. Reflect on the information and knowledge obtained.

In addition, Pappas (2014) has developed the following principles to help direct an inquiry-based assignment.

- Students are at the centre of the entire process, whereas teachers, resources, and technology are adequately organized to support them.
- All learning activities revolve around cognitive-processing skills (metacognition).
- Teachers observe the learning process in order to learn more about their students and the process of inquiry-based learning. Teachers intervene only to help students resolve misunderstandings and potential conflicts.
- Emphasis should be placed on helping students to assess the development of their cognitive-processing skills and conceptual understanding and not on the actual content of the field.

In higher education, inquiry-based assignments usually can be classified as one of the following four formats.

- *Confirmation inquiry*: Students are given a question, as well as a method, for which the result is already known. The goal is to confirm the result. This enables students to reinforce already established ideas and to practise their investigative skills.

- *Structured inquiry*: Students are given the question and the method of achieving the result, but the goal is to provide an explanation already supported by the evidence gathered during and through the investigative process.
- *Guided inquiry*: Students are given only a question. The main goal is to design the method of investigation and then test the question itself. This type of inquiry is not typically as structured as the previously mentioned forms.
- *Open inquiry*: Students must form their own questions, design investigative methods, and then carry out the inquiry itself. They must present their results at the end of the process.

Inquiry-based assignments can give teachers the opportunity to allow students to explore problems and scenarios fully so that they can learn from not only the results but also the process itself. They are encouraged to ask questions, explore their environments, obtain evidence that supports claims and results, and design convincing arguments regarding how they obtained their results.

Guidelines for Group Work

As highlighted in the Vaughan and Lee Wah (2020) study, students often express concerns about the division of labour and the quality of the process and product. In terms of the division of labour, students referred to the Pareto principle (Asad, 2013), according to which 20% of the group does 80% of the work. For example, one or two students end up doing the work while other group members contribute little or nothing. Moreover, in terms of quality, students commented on the challenge of being able to trust others and their level of work. It is important to provide students with guidelines to help them learn collaboratively to lead and direct their group work processes. We recommend the use of the following guidelines and frameworks for group work.

Group Learning Contracts

Group learning contracts can be used to direct group work. This can be a useful tool for helping students to plan and complete collaborative inquiry-based project work. These contracts also allow students to take active roles in setting the tone for group interaction and can help to "motivate ownership of learning" (Hesterman, 2016, p. 5). We recommend dedicating class time to the creation of a group learning contract. This way the teacher lets the students know that it is an important activity that merits time and attention. First, give the students time to reflect on and write down what they like and do not like about working in a group. Prompt them to consider their past experiences working in a group. What went well? What didn't go well? What contributed to the group's success or failure? What are their strengths when it comes to working collaboratively, and what is something that they would like to improve? Second, ask the students to sit down with their group members and share what they have written as a springboard to their discussion of ground rules and roles.

These contracts should be constructed by the students and reviewed by the teacher for constructive feedback and suggestions for modification. Both the students and the teacher should sign the final version of the learning contract. It then serves as an outline for the project and a tool to aid in the process of assessment. Modification of the learning contract might become necessary as the learning experience progresses. Modified contracts also should be approved and signed by both the students and the teacher. Failure of a student to meet the contract obligations can result in expulsion from the team. The following box is a sample learning contract adapted from the work of Knowles (1986).

Sample Learning Contract

Objectives: What are you going to learn?

- Itemize what you want to be able to *do* or *know* when completed.

Resources and strategies: How are you going to learn it?

- What do you have to *do* in order to meet each of the objectives defined?

Target date for completion: When do you plan to complete each task?

Evidence: How are you going to know that you learned it?

- What is the specific task that you are to complete to demonstrate learning?

Verification: How are you going to prove that you learned it?

- Who will receive the product of your learning, and how will they assess it?

Assessment: Teacher feedback.

- How well was the task completed? Provide an assessment decision.

In addition, both the University of Waterloo (2022b) and the Eberly Center at Carnegie Mellon University (2022) provide excellent examples of group learning contracts for use in higher education.

The ADDIE Model

The ADDIE model is an instructional design framework developed at Florida State University in the 1970s for the US military (Molenda, 2015). The model consists of the following five phases: analysis, design, development, implementation, and evaluation. This framework can be modified to guide an inquiry-based group project.

- *Analysis*: Start with a series of questions in order to clearly understand the goal and the context of the group work (triggering event).
- *Design*: Create a blueprint for the group project (exploration).
- *Development*: Develop and pilot the materials and resources for the group project (integration).
- *Implementation*: Present or implement the group project (application).
- *Evaluation*: Reflect on the group project process and create recommendations (resolution).

To use the ADDIE model effectively, we recommend that the teacher create groups with five student members. Each student is responsible for directing as well as reporting on the progress and completion of one of the five ADDIE phases. This allows all group members to take on a leadership role.

A RACI Matrix

A RACI matrix is a framework for defining and documenting roles and responsibilities for a group project (Kantor, 2018). Knowing exactly who is responsible, who is accountable, who needs to be consulted, and who must be kept informed at every step can significantly improve the quality of the group work process. RACI is an acronym for responsible, accountable, consulted, and informed.

- *Responsible*: This is the person responsible for performing and completing the task.
- *Accountable*: This is the person ultimately accountable for the task being done in a satisfactory manner. The accountable person must sign off on the work that the responsible person produces.
- *Consulted*: These are the people whose input is used to complete the task; communication with this group must be of a two-way nature.

- *Informed*: These are the people informed about the status of the task; communication with this group is of a one-way nature.

Once the student groups are formed, they collaborate to create a RACI matrix in an application such as Google Docs (Google, 2022a) or Google Sheets (Google, 2022g). This RACI matrix for an inquiry-based assignment indicates the project activities and deliverables and clearly illustrates the responsibilities for each group member for each task.

Product Activities/ Deliverables	Project Sponsor	Student 1	Student 2	Student 3	Student 4	Student 5
Create project charter	C	A	C	I	R	I
Create project plan/Gantt chart	I	A	R	C	R	I
Create business requirements	C	I	A	I	C	R
Create gap analysis	C	R	R	A	I	C
BPMN diagrams	I	R	C	C	A	C
Create recommendations	I	C	I	R	I	A

R = responsible, A = accountable, C = consulted, I = informed

This RACI matrix format shows all the tasks assigned to each student. This ensures that there is only one person accountable for any one task to avoid confusion. Typically, the list of objectives is in the left-hand column with the group member names across the top. Each work package is assigned to the appropriate project team member. The chart aids in communication among the project team members. In the example above, a Gantt chart is a bar chart that illustrates a project schedule and BPMN is the acronym for Business

Process Modeling Notation, which is an open standard to diagram a business process. Unfortunately, as Burns's (1785) poem about a mouse reminds us, "the best laid plans of mice and men often go astray" (seventh stanza). Even with the use of these guidelines for group work, conflict can arise inevitably. Initially, it is important to attempt to have the students resolve their own conflicts, but it is crucial that the teacher address these situations directly and resolve conflicts where necessary (Garrison, 2006). For example, the teacher can help to negotiate expectations or correct a student who is out of line (e.g., excessive or flaming online posts). It is important not to get involved directly in all these situations and mediate in a manner that encourages the students to address and resolve their own conflicts. If a conflict continues to escalate, then it is important to remind students in higher education that they must adhere to the institution's code of student conduct. We recommend placing a link in your blended course outline to your institution's code so that students are clear about the policy and the process for dealing with misconduct.

Conclusion

The teacher is the primary but not sole leader in a Community of Inquiry. Similar to a captain's responsibility for moving a ship forward, the teacher needs to encourage students to move beyond exploration to the integration and resolution phases of inquiry. As with facilitation, there is a delicate balance with direct instruction. Too much or too little direction from the teacher will adversely affect the engagement of students and their willingness to assume metacognitively the responsibilities of teaching presence. Direction in a Community of Inquiry is grounded in shared metacognition. That means being aware of intended goals and managing progression toward intended learning outcomes. Participants in a learning community must not only be aware metacognitively of the process of inquiry but also share thoughts regarding the positive development of collaborative inquiry. That is, learners must be prepared to offer direction that will move the discourse through to resolution in a timely manner. Consistent with the previous comments, metacognitively informed direction includes a strong assessment component, the focus of the next chapter.

5 | Assessment

We may not like it, but students can and do ignore our teaching; however, if they want to get a qualification, they have to participate in the assessment processes we design and implement.

—(Brown, 2004, p. 81)

The term "assessment" in higher education often conjures up different sentiments and emotions. From a teacher's perspective, Ramsden (2003, p. 180) states that assessment involves "getting to know our students and the quality of their learning." Conrad and Openo (2018) suggest that assessment fundamentally shapes approaches to learning and reveals the qualitative nature of the educational experience. Yet students in a research study were asked to use one word to describe their perceptions of assessment (Vaughan, 2013). The four most common words were *fear, stress, anxiety,* and *judgment.*

This disconnect between teacher and student perceptions regarding assessment is a serious issue, especially since a number of educational researchers have clearly linked student approaches to learning with the design and associated feedback of an assessment activity (Biggs, 1998; Hedberg & Corrent-Agostinho, 1999; Marton & Saljo, 1984;

Ramsden, 2003; Thistlethwaite, 2006). For example, standardized tests with minimal feedback can lead to memorization and a surface approach to learning, whereas collaborative group projects can encourage dialogue, richer forms of feedback, and deeper modes of learning (Entwistle, 2003). In addition, a report by the International Commission on the Futures of Education (2021) advocates that assessment needs to evolve from a mode of compliance to a process of shared goal setting, which leads to growth.

This focus on development is closely aligned with some Indigenous perspectives on assessment. Claypool and Preston (2011) state that Euro-American-centric assessment practices focus on written quizzes, tests, and exams, which primarily promote cognitive development via rational, linear, and accountable activities. They suggest that this approach to assessment is focused largely on meeting curricular outcomes, and it tends to neglect the physical, emotional, and spiritual domains of students. Marule (2012) suggests that effective assessment from an Indigenous perspective utilizes practices that include the cognitive domain but focus equally on physical, emotional, intellectual, and spiritual growth and development. Our seventh principle of blended learning, then, is ensuring that assessment is aligned with learning outcomes and growth for all students.

Our purpose in this chapter is to demonstrate how the Community of Inquiry framework can be applied to blended learning environments in order to encourage deep approaches to learning and create meaningful assessment activities for all students. The key is to maintain a CoI approach by not overloading students and teachers with assessment tasks (remember that less is more) as well as by providing choice and flexibility in the process of assessment.

Approaches to Assessment in Higher Education

In higher education, the three approaches to assessment commonly used by teachers are diagnostic, formative, and summative (Reeves, 2000). Diagnostic assessments are used to determine a student's prior knowledge and identify strengths and weaknesses. This type of self-assessment is crucial in helping students to become lifelong learners. As they engage in self-assessment practices, they learn to make sense of information, relate it to prior knowledge, and use it for new learning. This is often referred to in terms of assessment *as* learning since it helps students to develop and support their metacognitive skills (Manitoba Education, 2006). Diagnostic assessment is concerned with monitoring metacognitively the learning dynamic.

Formative assessment is used to provide students with feedback on their progress throughout a course. This type of assessment provides students with timely and specific feedback on how they might make adjustments to their learning. This assessment *for* learning approach can be accomplished through peer feedback techniques (LearnAlberta, 2008). This introduces the importance of shared metacognition to monitor the learning process, particularly to manage collaborative teaching and learning strategies going forward.

Summative assessment is used to estimate performance at the end of a course and to grade students' work. This assessment *of* learning is a snapshot in time that lets students know how well they have completed the learning tasks and activities. It provides information on their achievements (Manitoba Education, 2006).

Students develop a sense of ownership and efficacy when they use diagnostic, formative, and summative assessment feedback to make adjustments, improvements, and changes to how they learn and process information. These forms of assessment must be shared and discussed in order to foster a collaborative approach to learning.

In a blended learning environment, teachers can integrate these three forms of assessment in a purposeful and intentional manner.

Blended Approach to Assessment

As mentioned, a blended approach to learning and teaching provides opportunities to integrate meaningfully classroom and online learning opportunities. Diagnostic self-assessment approaches can be used to gauge student learning before a synchronous (face-to-face or F2F) session. Formative peer assessment techniques can be used for timely and specific feedback during anF2F session, and summative teacher assessments can be performed after an F2F session.

Diagnostic Self-Assessment: Before an F2F Session

Diagnostic self-assessment activities can be used as pre-class advance organizers to help teachers determine students' prior knowledge or experience with a concept, topic, or issue (Ausubel, 1968). These activities also help to engage students and stimulate existing connections with prior learning and experience. An excellent guide to creating pre-class diagnostic activities is Brame's (2013) website on just-in-time teaching.

This diagnostic assessment strategy was designed by Novak and colleagues (1999) as a feedback loop between pre-class and in-class activities. Students prepare for class by reading, viewing, or interacting with web-based resources and then complete an online diagnostic assessment activity (e.g., quiz, game, discussion forum post). Teachers have access to the compiled results from these diagnostic activities, which they can use to tailor the in-class (synchronous) activities to meet students' learning needs and expectations.

Pre-Class Readings and Videos

Probably the most common pre-class just-in-time teaching diagnostic activity is to have students read an article or watch a video and then complete a self-assessment quiz. In terms of readings, we recommend that teachers work with their subject area librarians to select peer-reviewed articles from their institutional online library resources (Mount Royal University, 2022). Doing so provides students with opportunities to practise their digital information literacy skills.

With regard to video, many teachers have taken their Microsoft PowerPoint (Microsoft, 2022) or Google Slides (Google, 2022f) presentations that traditionally they would have displayed during class time and created short, narrated versions for students to view before class. The key is to create a corresponding self-assessment quiz or knowledge probe that allows students to determine their prior knowledge and experience related to the key concepts, topics, or issues in the pre-class reading or video. These quizzes should focus on conceptual understanding rather than factual knowledge, and a final question should be included: "What did you not understand about the required reading or video, and what would you like us to focus on during our next class session?" These quizzes can be created easily by teachers in their institutional learning management systems, such as Blackboard (2022), Brightspace (Desire2Learn, 2022), Canvas (2022), and Moodle (2022).

TED-Ed Pre-Class Activities

In addition, the Technology, Entertainment, and Design (TED) non-profit organization has developed a free system for teachers to create pre-class activities using its extensive video repository (TED-Ed, 2022). Here is a sample process for creating these pre-class activities.

Process for Creating TED-Ed Pre-Class Activities

1. Create a free TED-Ed account. Go to ed.ted.com and click "Register" in the upper-right corner. This will allow you to create a username and password to manage all your activities and lessons.

2. Select a video for your pre-class activity. You can upload your own video, or visit the video search page to select a video by keyword, or paste in a YouTube URL (both public and unlisted YouTube videos work). Note that the videos here have not been filtered or vetted by the TED-Ed team, so make sure that you review the content of any video with which you are not familiar.

3. Create your pre-class activity.

   a. Customize one of TED-Ed's animations. You can also use any of the sample lessons provided in the public lesson library. To do so, visit any of the lesson pages in which you are interested, and use the red "Customize This Lesson" button at the bottom right to copy the lesson to your account. Keep any of the pre-populated questions and resources that you like, or feel free to add your own.

   b. If you are selecting a new video from YouTube, put the URL in the bar under "Create a Lesson." You'll be able to add an introduction to the video as well as the sections "Think" (multiple choice and open-ended questions), "Dig Deeper" (additional resources), and "Discuss" (guided or open forums).

4. Publish your pre-class activity (lesson). After you do so, you will receive a unique URL for your lesson page. Only you will have access to this link, and it is not listed in the site search on

ed.ted.com or indexed by search engines. However, anyone with whom you share this link will be able to access it, so you can share it with your class in whatever way works for you, such as via an institutional learning management system.

If you are adding a new video to the library, then when you publish it you can also choose to make it customizable, which means that others will be able to create their own lessons based upon the video that you have added.

5. Monitor student progress. As students submit work on your lesson (pre-class activity) page, you can monitor their progress and view their answers. You can manage the lessons that you have created, return to editing your drafts, or access student work at any time by visiting your lesson activity page.

Pre-Class Online Discussion Forum

An alternative to using online quizzes is an online discussion forum to allow students to post questions or issues related to the pre-class reading or video. This pre-class crowdsourcing can be a powerful learning activity because students are able to read and respond to each other's questions in advance of the F2F session.

In a blended course, the key to an effective online discussion is to link it clearly to the F2F session. For example, it is important for the teacher to review the discussion forum posts before class in order to determine key questions and themes, which can then be explored further, discussed, and debated during the synchronous session. We also recommend asking students for permission to display their posts during class time. Doing so helps to highlight key points and allows for an increased student "voice" in the synchronous discussions.

Digital Diagnostic Assessment Applications

With advances in digital technology, new forms of diagnostic assessment activities continue to emerge. For example, commercial software applications such as Lyryx (2022) have created sophisticated and challenging problems for students to solve before classes. Students receive immediate feedback on their problem-solving skills, and their results are automatically integrated into the learning management system's gradebook for teachers to view and compile for use in the F2F sessions.

Mobile phone apps have also provided opportunities for some creative diagnostic assessment activities. For example, Singapore Management University (2022) has developed an Accounting Challenge game app that students can play before a class session. There is an option to have students' game scores automatically entered into an institution's learning management system gradebook.

Our experience suggests that students often struggle with self-assessment activities in a blended course because of a lack of experience and proper instruction. Students in a related research study had a wide range of perceptions regarding the value of self-assessment (Vaughan, 2014). As one student indicated, "I don't find it too important to me. I see by my grades how I am doing instead of assessing myself" (Survey Participant 11); another student stated that "I would rather get feedback from a teacher or a peer" (Survey Participant 6). A number of students commented that they did not have previous experience with self-assessment activities; one noted that "I can sometimes have a hard time recognizing where I can improve when I'm self-assessing" (Survey Participant 17).

In terms of overcoming these issues, we recommend the Taylor Institute's (2022) Learning Module: Critical Reflection. This online resource provides faculty members with an extensive guide to designing, facilitating, and directing self-assessment activities in blended and online courses.

Formative Peer Assessment: During an F2F Session

A common complaint among students about a blended approach to learning is the-course-and-a-half syndrome (Twigg, 2003). They indicate that there is no clear connection or integration between the online and face-to-face components of a blended course and that they often feel like they are taking a course and a half. Thus, the key to a successful F2F session is to build upon student feedback collected from the pre-class diagnostic assessment activities.

Online Survey Results

Survey and quiz results or discussion forum posts can be shared by the teacher and reviewed by the students at the beginning of a class. The ensuing debate helps to clarify key concepts and allows students to begin comparing and contrasting their perspectives and experiences related to the questions and issues raised in the pre-class activities.

Formative Peer Assessment

Attributed to the French moralist and essayist Joubert (1842) is the quotation "to teach is to learn twice," and in an effective Community of Inquiry all participants are both students and teachers. The term "teaching" rather than "teacher" presence implies that everyone in the community is responsible for providing input on the design, facilitation, and direction of the teaching process. In a study conducted by Vaughan (2013), students commented on the value of formative peer assessment activities but indicated that one of the biggest challenges was finding a common place and time to meet outside the classroom. They recommended that teachers "provide class time to begin and conclude formative peer assessment activities in order to build trust and accountability for the peer assessment process" (p. 19).

Thomas and Brown (2021) have documented how the intentional design of formative assessment strategies helps to foster collaborative learning during synchronous sessions. They indicate that these designs include the use of conversational protocols to help students clarify their thinking. Such protocols are structured sets of guidelines to promote effective and efficient communication and problem solving (Government of Ontario, 2016). They also recommend creating class time for groups to engage in peer feedback loops in order to improve and refine their group work. This includes providing the groups with clear criteria (e.g., an assessment rubric) to give feedback to their peers. Loureiro et al. (2012) emphasize that clear criteria are essential to mitigate students' negative perceptions of peer assessment and support collaboration. Clarifying learning intentions helps to promote student success with collaborative learning activities (Wiliam & Leahy, 2015). The University of Wisconsin—Stout (2022) has an excellent online resource for creating and using rubrics for assessment.

Classroom Response Systems and Peer Instruction

The majority of students now have mobile phones, and they are being used as a classroom response system to support a form of peer instruction (Onodipe & Ayadi, 2020). The process begins with the teacher posing a question or problem. Such questions or problems should be focused on threshold concepts. Meyer and Land (2005) define a threshold concept as a core idea that is conceptually challenging for students. They often struggle to grasp it, but once grasped it radically transforms their perception of the subject. Although this material is difficult to learn, understanding threshold concepts is essential to mastering any field of study. Kent (2016) has created an excellent guide to the effective use of threshold concepts in higher education.

Once the teacher has displayed the question or problem digitally, the students work initially and individually toward a solution and vote on what they believe is the correct response by selecting the desired numbered or lettered response on their phones. The results are then projected for the entire class to view. For a good question, there is usually a broad range of responses. Students are then required to compare and discuss their solutions with the person next to them to reach a consensus (Salzer, 2018). Another vote is taken, but this time only one phone per group can be utilized. In most circumstances, the range of responses decreases and usually centres on the correct answer.

There are various software applications to support this form of peer instruction. Currently, three of the most common tools are Mentimeter (Menti, 2022), Poll Everywhere (2022), and Slido (2022), which have a variety of options and pricing requirements.

The use of classroom response systems and peer instruction is particularly effective in large classes at the beginning of a semester since it provides an "icebreaker" to allow students to get to know others in the course. After the initial activity, we recommend having students exchange email addresses or text message numbers so that they can begin the process of creating critical friends (described in Chapter 3).

Calibrated Peer Review

With regard to formative peer feedback, many students in higher education have limited prior experience, and often they are reluctant to engage meaningfully in this form of assessment practice (Vaughan, 2014). Therefore, it is important for teachers to provide students with guidance and practice on providing and receiving peer feedback. The University of California Los Angeles (2019) has developed the Calibrated Peer Review application to help students learn how to conduct a peer review.

Clase et al. (2010) describe the process as consisting of three phases.

1. *Writing*: Students first write and then digitally submit their work on a topic in a format specified by the teacher.
2. *Calibration training*: Training for peer review comes next. Students assess three "calibration" submissions against detailed questions that address the criteria on which the assignment is based. Students individually review each of these calibration

submissions according to the questions specified by the rubric and then assign a holistic rating out of 10. Feedback at this stage is vital. If the reviews are poorly done and do not yet meet the teacher's expectations, then the students get a second try. The quality of the reviews is taken into account in the next step of reviewing real submissions from other students.

3. *Peer review*: Once the deadline for calibration reviews has passed, each student is given anonymous submissions by three other students. The student uses the same rubric to review the peers' work, this time providing comments to justify the assessment and rating. Poor calibration performance in the second phase decreases the impact of the grades given to peers' work. After the students have done all three, they assess their own submissions.

A study by Pelaez (2002, p. 174) demonstrated how this peer review process helps students to improve their academic performance: "Results show that, when undergraduate non-science majors write about problem-based learning assignments followed by anonymous peer review, they perform better than with didactic lectures followed by group work."

Other web-based peer review systems include Kritik (2022) and Peergrade (2022). Kritik is an online peer assessment platform that focuses on learning by teaching. By using the application, "students who teach what they've learned go on to show higher levels of understanding and knowledge retention" (home page). Peergrade is also an online platform used to facilitate peer feedback sessions with students. Two research studies support the application's approach to peer feedback (Price et al., 2016; Sanchez et al., 2017). Both studies demonstrated that students who engaged in peer feedback activities performed better on subsequent tests and writing assignments than students who did not participate in such activities.

Labatorials

In our Introduction, we referred to Gierdowsk et al.'s (2020) study indicating that students want to continue face-to-face classes more than any other learning environment, with a majority preferring either completely or mostly F2F classes. To support a blended approach, Pelletier et al. (2021) describe how higher education institutions have begun to make major investments in classroom redesign for collaborative learning. One example is redesigning large lecture halls for labatorials (Sobhanzadeh & Zizler, 2021).

Typically, undergraduate courses in the natural sciences consist of lectures delivered by a tenured faculty member in a large hall with laboratory and tutorial sessions facilitated by graduate students. A common complaint from undergraduate students is the lack of alignment and clear connection between lectures and laboratory sessions. They also complain about the individualistic, formulaic, and repetitive nature of the laboratory assignments. To overcome these issues, the Department of Physics at the University of Calgary developed a modified labatorial approach (Ahrensmeier et al., 2009). Labatorials combine elements of both lab experiments and tutorials in order to allow students to develop their conceptual understanding of fundamental physics concepts through group-based problem solving and self-driven experimentation.

Labatorials are driven by a core experiment (or set of experiments). Students are asked to make predictions about the outcome, perform the experiment, collect data, and interpret the results (Kalman et al., 2020). Students might be given direct instructions for some experimental parts of the lab, whereas for other parts they might be asked to design their own simple protocols for investigating the concept at hand. Labatorials focus on key physics concepts and encourage students to present and share their ideas with one another. After performing the experiments, they discuss whether or not the results support their hypotheses. There are typically three to six checkpoints in each labatorial to encourage ongoing interaction between the students and the teaching team, consisting of faculty members and graduate students. Each time the students reach a checkpoint, they review the answers with the teaching team. All students in one group must have the same answers. If the answer to a question is wrong, or students are not proceeding in the right direction, then the teaching team directs them to find the correct answer by themselves, exploring and discussing alternative ideas.

In a labatorial, students can work collaboratively at circular tables with whiteboards and projection screens on the walls. The whiteboards can be used for collaborative problem solving, and the projection screens can be used to display student work to the entire class. For more information on classroom redesign for blended learning, we recommend the Western Active Learning Spaces website (University of Western Ontario, 2022).

Teacher Assessment: After an F2F Session

Teacher assessment practices in higher education are often limited to high-stakes summative assessment activities such as midterm and final examinations (Boud, 2000). The role of a teacher in a Community of Inquiry is to provide ongoing and meaningful assessment feedback in order to help students develop the necessary metacognitive skills and strategies to take responsibility for their own learning.

Video Feedback

In a blended environment, there are a variety of digital technologies that a teacher can use to provide diagnostic, formative, and summative assessments to students in a Community of Inquiry. For example, teachers can use collaborative writing tools such as Google Docs (Google, 2022a) to provide formative assessment feedback at checkpoints or milestones for individual or group projects. This approach allows students to receive teacher feedback throughout the process of constructing the project rather than just focusing on summative assessment feedback on the final product.

In addition, teachers can use digital video to provide assessment feedback. Ryan (2021) has published a paper describing how video feedback can be used to support the socio-emotional aspects of blended and online learning. She recommends the following key design considerations for creating video feedback comments in order to bolster socio-emotional outcomes for students.

Different from text-based feedback. Video feedback can and should feature messages qualitatively different from text-based feedback. Content analysis conducted by Borup et al. (2015) showed that text-based feedback tended to feature comments that highlighted specific strengths, weaknesses, and areas for improvement in relation to the task. In contrast, video feedback more frequently included general and specific praise for the students' work as well as comments aimed at strengthening the relationship between teacher and student (e.g., use of the student's name). As shown in the broader feedback and blended learning literature, both praise and relational comments are useful for improving social presence, strengthening feelings of trust, and helping students to feel supported and motivated (Plante & Asselin, 2014; Yang & Carless, 2013).

Time-sensitive nature of video feedback. Borup et al. (2015) and others (e.g., Crow & Murray, 2020) argue that it is important for teachers to foster a sense of community and belonging in the first few weeks of the semester. Furthermore, students can obtain a greater sense of value, support, and social presence when feedback on assessment tasks is provided in a timely manner (Crow & Murray, 2020; Plante & Asselin, 2014).

Video feedback can be more effective for certain types of students. For example, students who are generally moderate-to-high achievers but have performed poorly on an assessment task during the COVID-19 pandemic (presumably because of health or well-being issues) can benefit from the more personalized and supportive style of communication that video feedback affords. In these circumstances, Borup et al. (2015) argue that it is important for teachers to be highly cognizant of keeping their body language, expression, and tone of voice positive so as not to convey unintentionally information that could be interpreted as negative or discouraging.

Caldwell (2021) reverses this process and requires students to create videos to demonstrate their conceptual understanding of first-year physics principles. This process begins early in the course (e.g., the first question on the first assignment). She asks students to upload short videos introducing themselves to the class. They are free to share whatever information they wish in these videos. Their purpose is to build community and have students learn the process of recording and uploading a video to the learning management system. Caldwell indicates that she posts an instructional video to demonstrate the upload process, but invariably there are some technical issues for students to work out (e.g., certain devices can upload videos only by using certain web browsers). She recommends that it is best to sort out these issues early in the course, before students become too busy with the actual course work.

Then, throughout her first-year physics course, Caldwell (2021) has one video explanation question on each assignment. She emphasizes that the types of questions that she assigns for video explanation are not typical calculation problems from a physics textbook but focused on an explanation of the steps behind the calculation. She also provides the following example of asking students to do the following.

- List the forces that act on the person, and classify them as conservative or non-conservative.
- Explain whether mechanical energy is conserved based on the specific criteria I provide.

- Show how trigonometry can be used to calculate the relevant distances.
- Find the minimum speed the person must be running to make it across the ravine.

Flipgrid (2022) is a free web-based video discussion platform from Microsoft that can be particularly effective for this type of assessment process. This application allows teachers or students to post a discussion prompt, and then other students can respond with short videos.

Flipgrid Video Assessment Process

1. *Create a topic.* Teachers and students need to create a free educator account at Flipgrid.com. The first step is to create a topic. A topic is a discussion prompt for the assessment activity.

   Write a prompt and include anything that you would like students to review prior to responding, such as videos and links.

   Flipgrid has a Discovery Library with thousands of age- and subject-specific topic prompts that you can use in your blended course.

2. *Set access and share.* After creating your topic, choose how students will access it. If they have institutional email addresses, add the domain (everything after the @ symbol in their email addresses). If your students do not have institutional email addresses, then create a username for each student.

   Share your topic by using one of the share buttons (Google Classroom, Microsoft Teams) or copy and paste the unique join code however you connect with the students in your blended course.

3. *Students respond.* After entering your join code, students gain access by logging in via email or username.

Students share their voices by recording short videos with Flipgrid's camera. Flipgrid contains a variety of tools for students to tell their stories, including text, emoji, inking, boards, screen recording, the ability to upload clips, and more.

Community Expert Assessment Activities

Digital technologies also provide opportunities for students to receive assessment feedback from experts in a field of study. This can be accomplished through the use of blogs, videos, and professional learning plans.

Blogs

For example, students are often required to critique academic articles on key concepts and findings in a disciplinary field of study. Students often find this type of assignment tedious since they find the articles challenging to read, and they receive limited feedback on their critiques. To improve the effectiveness of this critique assignment, we recommend that teachers work in partnership with their instructional librarians first to identify seminal articles and second to contact the authors of the articles and invite them to review the students' critiques.

We then recommend the following process to guide the article critique and review process. Be sure to provide students with a clear rationale for the assignment as well as samples of previous work, an assessment rubric, and a guide to writing an article critique. We recommend providing students with an opportunity to use the assessment rubric to review collaboratively previous work so that they are clear about the expectations of the assignment. The University of Arizona (2022) also has an excellent student guide to writing an article critique.

1. *Initial article critique*: Students use a blogging application such as Blogger (2022) or WordPress (2022) to compose the first draft of the critique.

2. *Peer review*: The teacher then provides time during the synchronous session for these drafts to be peer reviewed by critical friends.

3. *Author review*: The student revises the critique based upon the peer review, and then the author of the article is invited to provide an expert review of the student's work.

4. *Teacher review*: The student makes final revisions to the critique based upon the author's review and submits the final work to the teacher for a summative assessment.

Students who have completed an article critique with author feedback commented that publishing their critiques and receiving expert feedback made the task much more authentic and engaging.

Videos

Community experts can also provide assessment feedback on individual or group presentations through the use of web-based video technologies. These types of presentations can be video-recorded and either streamed live (e.g., Vimeo, 2022) or posted to a video-sharing site such as YouTube (2022). The community experts can then provide assessment feedback to the students in either synchronous (e.g., real-time audio) or asynchronous formats (e.g., online discussion forums).

E-Portfolios

Teachers are also encouraged to take a portfolio approach to assessment in their courses and programs. This involves students receiving peer, self-, and teacher assessments on their course assignments. For example, students complete the first draft of a course assignment and post it to their e-portfolios. The critical friends then review the assignments and provide peer feedback. Students use this feedback to improve the quality of their work, and they have the opportunity for external experts to provide them with additional feedback. The students then complete self-assessments to ensure that they have met all the objectives of the course assignment. Finally, the teacher reviews the course assignment and provides summative assessment feedback.

Various e-portfolio tools can support this process, ranging from commercial applications such as Weebly (2022) and Wix (2022) to the free Google Sites tool (Google, 2022e). The teacher education program at Mount Royal University (MRU) uses e-portfolios to support a professional learning plan process modelled on the Alberta Teachers Association (2022) professional growth plan. An MRU teacher candidate's professional learning plan is the primary space in which a student can document and articulate learning related to the MRU Bachelor of Education program competencies (planning, facilitating, assessing, inclusive environment, professional roles and responsibilities). This is the space in which teacher candidates can develop and communicate self-understanding and create learning goals that allow them to be successful in their future teaching practice.

In addition, Mitchell et al. (2021) have documented how an e-portfolio approach to assessment can greatly enhance student employability. They conducted a research study at Griffith University in Australia in which students indicated that e-portfolios could have a positive impact on their employability by allowing them to demonstrate their learning as well as assisting them in their professional development. The students in this study further stated that the most beneficial aspects of ePortfolios related to employability were the ability to collate experiences and assessments, provide evidence of competency development, and facilitate reflection in order to help them develop a "growth mindset" (Dweck, 2006).

Classroom Assessment Techniques

As we indicated in Chapter 2, it is important that the design and organization of a blended course are flexible in order to meet the emerging learning needs and interests of students throughout the semester. In addition, students in a teacher education study wanted to "provide teachers with more feedback on their assignments and teaching practice throughout the semester, not just at the end—assessment should be a two-way conversation between students and instructors" (Vaughan, 2010, p. 22). We recommend the use of classroom assessment techniques as a method for teachers to receive ongoing feedback from students about the course design.

The Classroom Assessment Techniques (CATs) approach was developed by Angelo and Cross (1993). They are simple, non-graded, anonymous activities designed to allow students to provide faculty members with feedback about the teaching-learning process in a course. The following box highlights some of the most common CATs.

Common Classroom Assessment Techniques

Minute Paper

The minute paper assesses if and how students gain knowledge. The teacher finishes a synchronous session by asking the students to use a digital quiz tool such as Google Forms (Google, 2022b) to write a brief response to the following questions: "What was the most important thing you learned during this class?" and "What important question remains unanswered?" The teacher can then share the results digitally with the entire class and discuss key themes and issues in the next synchronous session.

Muddiest Point

The muddiest point is one of the simplest CATs to help assess where students are having difficulties. The technique consists of asking them to use a digital quiz application to jot down quick responses to one question: "What was the muddiest point in [the lecture, discussion, homework assignment, film, etc.]?" The term "muddiest" means "most unclear" or "most confusing." Again the teacher can share the results digitally with the entire class and discuss key themes and issues in the next synchronous session.

What's the Principle?

This CAT is useful in courses requiring problem solving. After students figure out what type of problem they are dealing with, often they must decide which principle(s) to apply in order to solve the problem. This CAT provides students with a few problems and asks them to state the principle that best applies to each problem, using either a classroom response system (e.g., a voting app) or a digital quiz application. It is important that the teacher immediately share the results with the students during the synchronous session for clarification and discussion.

Defining Features Matrix

For this CAT, the teacher needs to prepare a digital handout (e.g., Google Docs) that has a matrix of three columns and a row for each student in the class. At the top of the first two columns, list two distinct concepts that have potentially confusing similarities (e.g., hurricanes versus tornadoes, Picasso versus Matisse). In the third column, list the important characteristics of both concepts in no particular order. Then ask students to use this matrix anonymously during class time to identify which characteristics belong to each of the two concepts. Review the responses as an entire class in order to understand and diagnose with which characteristics the students are struggling.

In a blended course, CATs are particularly effective since they demonstrate to students that teaching presence is an ongoing process of inquiry, experimentation, and reflection. They also provide concrete evidence that the teacher cares about the learning process.

Course Evaluation

Although the terms "assessment" and "evaluation" occasionally have been used synonymously, there is an important difference (Garrison, 2017). Assessment is associated with determining students' learning processes and outcomes, whereas evaluation is used to refer to the act of comparing a unit, course, or program with some set of performance or outcome criteria.

Evaluation begins by determining the strategic intent of the course or program. In this regard, clearly identifying why a particular course has been redesigned for blended learning is crucial to evaluating its effectiveness. Traditionally, distance education courses have been offered in order to increase access to educational opportunities by spanning geographic or temporal distances. Although access is a component of blended learning, added value speaks to issues of quality reflected by collaborative thinking and learning experiences. To evaluate this type of blended learning experience, we recommend using the Community of Inquiry (Garrison et al., 2022) and Shared Metacognition (Garrison & Akyol, 2015a) surveys.

With regard to the CoI survey, Arbaugh et al. (2008) conducted a multi-institutional study to develop and validate this survey instrument, which operationalizes Garrison et al.'s (2000) CoI framework. The results of their research suggest that the instrument is a valid, reliable, and efficient measure of the dimensions of social presence and cognitive presence, thereby providing additional support for the validity of the CoI framework in constructing effective online learning environments. Although factor analysis supported the idea of teaching presence as a construct, it also suggested that the construct consisted of two factors: one related to course design and organization, the other related to instructor behaviour during the course.

The CoI survey has been used extensively to evaluate the social presence, cognitive presence, and aspects of teaching presence for numerous online and blended courses. More information on the CoI survey can be found on the CoI website (Garrison et al., 2022), and the survey questions are listed in Appendix D. In addition, Garrison and Akyol (2015a) conducted a research study to develop and validate a shared metacognitive construct and questionnaire for use in collaborative learning environments. The questionnaire was developed using the CoI framework as a theoretical guide and tested by applying qualitative research techniques. The results indicate that, in order to understand better the structure and dynamics of metacognition in emerging collaborative learning environments, we must go beyond individual approaches to learning and consider metacognition in terms of complementary self-regulation and co-regulation that integrate individual and shared regulation.

We recommend shared metacognition as an area of study for those interested in thinking and learning collaboratively in blended courses and programs. Shared metacognition provides the construct to study how students manage discourse actively and construct meaning responsibly. The construct provides a solid theoretical foundation and an instrument to explore the complex transaction of a Community of Inquiry. Additional information on the shared metacognition survey is contained in a blog post by Garrison (2019), and the survey questions can be found in Appendix E.

We encourage the combined use of the shared metacognition and CoI surveys in order to study the design, facilitation, and direction of shared metacognition in a blended Community of Inquiry. An example of how to do this is provided in a study by Vaughan and Lee Wah (2020), who examined the development of shared metacognition in a blended teacher education course.

Conclusion

In a blended Community of Inquiry, self-, peer, and teacher assessments should be an integrated process rather than a series of isolated events in order to help all students develop shared metacognitive awareness and strategies. For example, a student in a teacher education study commented that "I used self-reflection for checking my work and making sure I had everything I needed. I used peer-review for a different perspective on my work, and I used teacher feedback to understand how I could improve my work" (Vaughan, 2010, p. 23). Another student in the study stated that "self-reflection showed me what I liked about my work and what needed to be improved, peer feedback gave comments on what could be done better and then teacher feedback gave ideas on how the assignment could be fixed up to get a better mark" (p. 23).

In addition, these students stressed how a blended CoI framework supported by digital technologies helped them to integrate these three forms of assessment into a triad approach (see Figure 5.1).

This triad approach involves students using rubrics, blogs, and online quizzes to provide themselves with self-reflection and feedback on their course assignments. They can then receive further peer feedback on their course work via digital technologies such as classroom response systems and calibrated peer review tools. Finally, teachers and, in some cases, community experts can review students' e-portfolios and use digital video technologies to observe student performance, diagnose student misconceptions, and provide additional assessment feedback.

An international call for a greater focus on assessment for learning, rather than on assessment for just measurement and accountability of student performance, is well documented in the educational research literature (Yeh, 2009). The use of digital technologies to

Figure 5.1

Using Digital Technologies to Support a Triad Approach to Assessment in a Blended Course

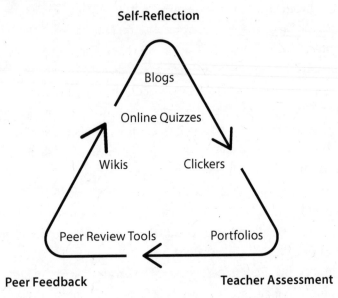

support student assessment in a blended Community of Inquiry can lead to Hattie's (2009, p. 238) vision of a visible teaching and learning framework in which "teachers SEE learning through the eyes of their students and students SEE themselves as their own teachers."

6 | Leading Collaboratively

Collaborative leadership pulls together leaders at all levels of the institution. It means encouraging input and creating ownership through collaboratively developing a vision and plan as well as sharing responsibility for the outcomes.

—(Garrison, 2016, p. 146)

As educational institutions face tremendous winds of change, their traditional hierarchical approach to leadership is proving to be less effective in dealing with those changes. Not only is higher education in need of commitment to change, but also there is a need for a new kind of leadership. It will create structures and processes that engage individuals across the organization. Leading collaboratively creates an organizational culture in which leadership is a shared responsibility (Garrison, 2016). Collaborative inquiry focused on leadership necessitates an investment in the culture of the organization that reflects a climate of trust, shared responsibility, and clear direction.

Fernandez and Shaw (2020) document how the decision to pivot to remote learning during the COVID-19 pandemic was made swiftly. Moreover, they note that institutions operating with a shared leadership model benefited from a greater degree of agility, innovation, and collaboration. They also highlight three best practices for leadership for navigating unpredictable challenges such as the pandemic. First, they discuss a form of servant leadership that emphasizes empowerment, involvement, and collaboration in which academic leaders place the interests of others above their own. Second, they recommend that academic leaders distribute leadership responsibilities, including a measure of authority to make decisions, to a network of teams throughout the organization to improve the quality of the decisions made in resolving crises. And third, they advocate that leaders communicate clearly and frequently with all stakeholders through a variety of channels. With regard to the third recommendation, Schrage (1995, p. 5) adds that "organizations that attempt to substitute increased communication for increased collaboration will learn the hard way that there is a tremendous difference. Flooding someone with more information doesn't necessarily make him a better thinker." This thinking is akin to Freire's (2018) argument for applying a problem-solving approach (shared discourse), which includes effective two-way communication, rather than a banking model (depositing information) to higher education. In addition, we emphasize that there is an important difference between cooperation and collaboration. Cooperation in an organization too often means that individuals are to do their jobs without concern about the bigger picture. Collaboration means working with others on common problems or innovations such as blended learning (Garrison, 2017). Effective groups are distinguished by "members who communicated a lot, participated equally, and possessed good emotion-reading skills" (Woolley et al., 2015, third last paragraph).

Brown (2021) refers to this as a form of integrated leadership. He suggests that integration is the key driver of digital transformation in higher education. No single unit, not even the president's office, can accomplish this transformation by itself. Brown believes that such transformation calls for "deep and coordinated shifts within an institution and that coordination implies integration" (p. 43). He states that integration begins with and is propelled by leadership, especially leadership that "sets aside turf battles and instead forms collaborative, cross-institutional partnerships to achieve . . . goals [of digital transformation]" (p. 43).

This concept of integrated leadership aligns closely with Indigenous principles of educational leadership. These principles consist of cultural awareness, collaboration, and capacity building (Morin, 2016). In terms of cultural awareness, Schein (2011, p. 354) indicates that "culture is pervasive; it influences all aspects of how an organization deals with its primary task, its various environments, and its internal operations." With regard to an Indigenous educational context, leaders need to stand back and observe the community and school culture. Stockdale et al. (2013, p. 99) found that "highly effective First Nations principals take the time to really 'know' the community and are comfortable attending community functions."

Morin (2016) emphasizes the importance of an Indigenous leader's ability to bring people together and support collaboration with one another. She stresses that leaders need to put their differences aside as they team up with their colleagues to figure out a solution to a problem, such as low school attendance and engagement. Gurr et al. (2006, p. 382) states that effective leaders "clear a pathway for people to be involved and achieve [results] by removing blockages and providing a clear vision serviced by adequate resources."

In terms of capacity building, Indigenous leadership involves taking risks and making changes (Morin, 2016). A case study by Mulford et al., (2007, p. 22) identified that capacity building consists of a three-stage process through which leaders who supported and encouraged their staff "encouraged others to undertake leadership roles, encouraged staff to accept responsibility for their professional learning, and fostered and supported professional learning for groups (for example, senior staff)."

Initiating and Sustaining Organizational Change

Collaborative or integrative leadership allows organizations to initiate, respond to, and sustain change. As we have documented in this book, the learning experience in higher education is focused increasingly on blending face-to-face and online learning (Pelletier et al., 2021). Although blended learning course redesigns are becoming common in higher education, few are grounded in a strategic institutional initiative with policy and financial support from senior administration. Too often they are seen as "one-off" course projects associated with unwanted technology innovation. For this reason, it is clear that transformation must be framed as an institutional strategy with collaborative and visible leadership.

Garrison and Kanuka (2004, pp. 102–103) offer a list of blended learning course redesign requirements to be sustainable.

- Create a clear institutional direction and policy.
- Frame the potential, increase awareness, and commit.
- Establish a single point of support, quality assurance, and project management.
- Create an innovation fund to provide the financial support and incentives to faculty and departments to initiate blended learning course transformations.
- Invest in a reliable and accessible technology infrastructure.
- Strategically select prototype projects that prove to be exceptionally successful exemplars of effective learning.
- Develop formal instructional design support available through a blended format.
- Systematically evaluate satisfaction and success of the teaching, learning, technology, and administration of new courses.
- Create a task group to address issues, challenges, and opportunities and communicate and recommend new directions to the university community.

Examples of higher education institutions that have followed these guidelines include the University of Ottawa, the University of Central Florida, and the University of Wisconsin—Madison. At the University of Ottawa, the Board of Governors approved an initiative for the implementation of large-scale blended courses in April 2013 led by the vice-provost of teaching and learning. As part of this initiative, the university established the goal of converting 20% of its course offerings, roughly 1,000 courses, into a blended format. This transformation affected 500 professors and close to 25,000 students. An interim report indicated that the University of Ottawa was on track to achieve this goal, and its success was attributed to the collaborative leadership approach by the institution's Teaching Learning Support Services (2016).

The University of Central Florida began its blended learning initiative in 1996, and the majority of its courses are now offered in a blended format. Similar to the University of Ottawa, the University of Central Florida credits the success of its blended learning initiative to collaborative leadership as well as its Research Initiative for Teaching Effectiveness team. That team is dedicated to assessing and communicating the impacts of instructional technologies on the learning climate of the university (Research Initiative for Teaching Effectiveness, 2022).

Another pioneer in the field of blended learning is the University of Wisconsin—Madison. It, too, has developed an overarching collaborative vision of its institutional blended learning initiative, but each school, college, institute, and division has created its own disciplinary vision of blended learning and created its own campus toolkit (University of Wisconsin—Madison, 2022). Such web-based toolkits provide each discipline with a place to share its stories, resources, and events with its community of users.

Faculty Development

Pelletier et al. (2021) indicate that one of the biggest challenges to the successful adoption of blended learning in higher education is effective faculty development programs. Unfortunately, the faculty culture in higher education is experiencing an erosion of collaboration and community (Picciano, 2021). For significant and sustained change in blended teaching and learning, faculty must have opportunities for, and be supported in, working collaboratively as trusted colleagues rather than simply attending a series of "one-off" educational technology workshops (Garrison, 2016; Smadi et al., 2021b). A study by Waghid et al. (2021) demonstrated how a coherent framework such as the Community of Inquiry could be used effectively to guide faculty development for blended and online learning. The findings from this study were echoed by Pischetola (2021), who stressed how important use of the CoI framework was in helping faculty to redesign their courses for blended learning.

The University of Calgary developed a course redesign program for blended learning based upon the CoI framework called the Inquiry through Blended Learning (ITBL) program (Vaughan, 2010). The focus of inquiry in the program was on the connection between one's teaching practice and student learning. The potential exists in such a professional development program for faculty to make a transformational shift in their approach to teaching from disseminating information to creating learning environments. Students co-construct their knowledge through interactions with the professor, their peers, and the course content. The role of technology shifts from the packaging and distribution of information content to its use as a "toolkit" to enable students to communicate and construct collaboratively their own knowledge. Technology can be used as a catalyst (triggering event) to question one's curriculum and pedagogy (Sands, 2002).

By applying the CoI framework to the ITBL program, the focus of the cognitive presence sphere became a process of inquiry into teaching practice (Vaughan & Garrison, 2005). The ability of the community to support and sustain this inquiry formed the social presence. The opportunities for blended (face-to-face and online learning) support were encapsulated within the teaching presence. Figure 6.1 and the box below illustrate how the CoI framework was adapted for a blended faculty development initiative.

Figure 6.1
Blended Faculty Community of Inquiry—Three Presences

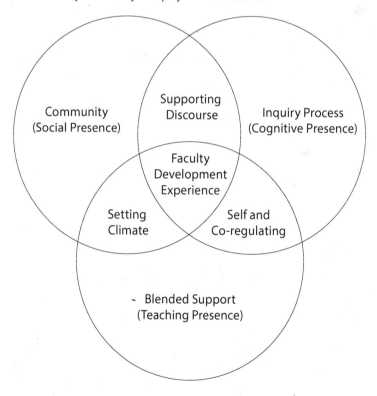

Inquiry Process

As discussed in Chapter 1, cognitive presence is the element of the CoI framework most basic to success in higher education. Cognitive processes and outcomes should be the focus of an educational Community of Inquiry, so social presence and even teaching presence are facilitators of that learning process. Garrison and Anderson (2003, p. 55) state that "cognitive presence means facilitating the analysis, construction, and confirmation of meaning and understanding in a community of learners through sustained discourse and reflection."

Categories and Indicators of a Blended Faculty Community of Inquiry

Inquiry process (cognitive presence) is the extent to which faculty can construct and confirm meaning through sustained reflection, discourse, and application in a blended Community of Inquiry. The phases move from triggering event to exploration to integration to resolution/application. The indicators include

- inciting curiosity and defining key questions or issues for investigation;
- exchanging and exploring perspectives and information resources with faculty colleagues;
- connecting ideas through individual project construction; and
- applying new ideas directly in teaching practice.

Community (social presence) is the ability of faculty in a blended Community of Inquiry to project themselves socially and emotionally as real people (i.e., their full personalities) through the medium of communication used. Faculty learn best from each other. The phases move from establishing trust and respect to open communication to group cohesion. The indicators include expressing emotion, engaging in risk-free expression, and fostering collaboration.

Blended support (teaching presence) is the design, facilitation, and direction of the inquiry and community processes for the purpose of realizing personally meaningful and educationally worthwhile learning outcomes for faculty in an environment that carefully integrates face-to-face and online sessions and activities. The categories include

- organizing and designing the faculty development program;
- facilitating discourse in the community; and
- providing direct instruction for faculty participants.

The indicators include

- setting curriculums and methods;
- stimulating and sustaining the sharing of personal meanings and insights; and
- modelling and focusing discussion, activities, and project construction.

To recap, cognitive presence is linked closely to the concept of critical thinking derived from Dewey's (1933) reflective thinking and Practical Inquiry model. According to Dewey, practical inquiry is grounded in experience and integrates the public and private worlds of the learner. Based upon this definition, Garrison et al. (2000) developed their PI model to guide the analysis of cognitive presence in an educational experience mediated by computer conferencing. The four categories of this model—triggering event, exploration, integration, and resolution—were used to guide the process of inquiry in the ITBL program.

Triggering Event

A triggering event, as described by Garrison et al. (2000, p. 21), is a "state of dissonance or feeling of unease resulting from an experience." Discussions with faculty indicate that the triggering event for participation in the ITBL program was the motivation to redesign an existing course to improve student learning and faculty satisfaction. This desire presents the opportunity to make one's implicit assumptions about a particular course design explicit. The ITBL course redesign process was initiated through a formal call for proposals to participate in a blended faculty Community of Inquiry. The application process was designed so that faculty were provided with the CoI framework and the necessary support to begin reflecting on their existing courses and making initial plans for the process of redesigning them.

The ITBL application form consisted of three parts: project detail, project evaluation and sustainability plans, and proposed budget. A series of brown-bag lunches and one-on-one application consultation sessions was also provided to ensure that faculty were clear about the course redesign focus of the program and the expectation that they would become active participants in the blended faculty development Community of Inquiry. Inherent in this process, faculty were encouraged to take a community or team approach to the redesign process in their applications. These teams often consisted of a group of faculty who taught the selected course as well as teaching assistants, graduate students, and others who provided course-related support (e.g., subject area librarians).

Once the successful ITBL applicants were informed of their awards, an initial project meeting was scheduled that included the project team (faculty, teaching assistants, graduate students) and representatives from the institution's teaching and learning centre, library, and information technology department. The purpose of this meeting was to clarify the project goals, timelines, roles, and responsibilities for those involved in supporting the redesign process. This meeting also helped to identify professional development support needs and requirements for the project team members. This information was then used to shape the activities and resources incorporated into the ITBL program.

As a follow-up to this meeting, the project teams were encouraged to post a summary message to a discussion board on a course website that had been constructed for the ITBL program. The message described the course redesign goals for the project, action plans, and any questions related to the redesign process (triggering events). Besides helping to clarify the course redesign process, the post allowed the other members of the ITBL cohort to begin to learn more about each other's project. This discussion forum posting process also provided the first hands-on opportunity for the participants to interact as students with the learning management system used in most cases in their own programs.

The first face-to-face ITBL cohort meeting was designed to build upon the initial discussion forum posts to allow the participants to discuss further their course redesign questions and trigger new ideas and perspectives about teaching and learning. This process was facilitated by selectively placing the participants into small groups so that they had opportunities to interact with people from the other project teams. The three questions used to stimulate the discussion were as follows.

- What is your definition of blended learning, and how will this concept be operationalized in your course redesign project?
- What will be the advantages (for both students and professors) of your course redesign?
- What do you perceive will be some of the challenges that you will encounter with your project?

An instructional design or teaching specialist was placed at each table to help guide the small group discussions and subsequently record the key points. These discussion summaries were then posted on the ITBL website as a resource and "touchstone" to stimulate further online discussion.

Our experience suggests that the initial face-to-face cohort meetings were very important in establishing the blended faculty Community of Inquiry (Vaughan & Garrison, 2006). Through the discussions in these meetings, the community members realized that they were not alone in experiencing a particular course redesign issue or concern. This shared understanding and the physical presence of the meetings quickly led to a sense of "trust and risk taking" in the group.

Exploration

The second phase of the PI model is exploration, characterized by "searching for clarification and attempting to orient one's attention" (Garrison et al., 2000, p. 21). The exploration phase of the ITBL program consisted of a series of integrated face-to-face and online experiential learning activities that allowed the participants to become immersed in a blended learning environment from a student's perspective. This process took place over an extended period of time, a minimum of six months, and the activities were developed based upon the feedback from the initial project meetings and in collaboration with the faculty participants of the program. These ITBL program activities were designed to provide participants with experience and expertise in the areas of curriculum design, teaching strategies, and educational technology integration (see Figure 6.2).

The curriculum design sphere involved the creation of a course outline or syllabus for the blended learning course. This document became the "blueprint" for the redesign process. In terms of teaching strategies, the ITBL program provided opportunities for the participants to develop experience and skill with online discussions, group work, and computer-mediated assessment practices. The educational technology integration component involved the acquisition of strategies

Figure 6.2

ITBL Program Outcomes for the Faculty Participants

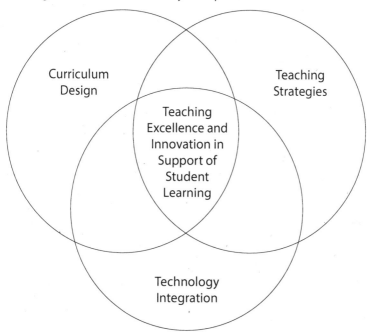

Curriculum Design

Teaching Strategies

Teaching Excellence and Innovation in Support of Student Learning

Technology Integration

and skills for managing a course website and troubleshooting basic student technology issues.

To achieve these program outcomes, a variety of learning opportunities allowed the participants to share, discuss, and debate their course redesign experiences (Garrison & Vaughan, 2008). In the ITBL program, various information and communication technologies were used to support the exploration phase. For example, Adobe Connect was used to create brief audio presentations to help the participants prepare for upcoming face-to-face sessions, explain online activities, and summarize key course redesign concepts. Faculty research and travel commitments meant that not everyone could attend each regular face-to-face session. To overcome this challenge, a web-based synchronous communication tool similar to Zoom was used to record the face-to-face sessions for future use. A web-based conferencing application was also used to support "virtual" project meetings when team members were off campus.

In addition, faculty mentors (professors with previous blended learning experience) and students were included in the ITBL discussions. The students provided the all-important perspective of the learner (the target audience for the redesigned courses), and the faculty mentors were able to pass on their "lessons learned" from direct experience with inquiry and blended learning courses. Previous participants in the ITBL program also stressed the importance of conducting these discussions in both face-to-face and online formats (Vaughan & Garrison, 2005). The face-to-face sessions, with their physical presence and sense of immediacy, helped to establish the rhythm for the community, and the online discussion forums allowed for reflective thoughts and comments to be captured and archived as project-related resources.

Integration

The third phase is integration, which involves reflecting on how the new information and knowledge discovered can be integrated into a coherent idea or concept (Garrison et al., 2000). A common challenge for the participants involved in the ITBL program was the transition from the exploration phase to the integration phase. Many faculty members were comfortable sharing, discussing, and debating course redesign concepts, but a greater effort often was required to transfer these new ideas into practice. One strategy used in the ITBL program involved getting faculty to present project artifacts regularly, such as their course outline or assessment activity, to the rest of the community. This forced the ITBL participants to make redesign decisions and to create course-related resources. This "show and tell" process also allowed them to get valuable feedback from their peers on the artifacts. In addition, opportunities were provided to pilot portions of the projects with students who could provide insightful comments on the usability and educational value of a learning activity or resource.

To support the integration phase further, a series of individual project meetings was conducted outside the regular ITBL cohort activities. These meetings were facilitated by an instructional design or teaching specialist assigned to specific projects based upon areas of expertise that correlate to the predetermined support requirements for the project. The frequency and scope of these meetings depended on the needs of each project. Although the larger cohort meetings provided opportunities for the participants to be exposed to a diversity of ideas, these meetings focused on "getting things done." Project development work and milestones were reviewed at each meeting, with tasks and "deliverables" assigned for the subsequent meeting.

Application/Resolution

Resolution of the dilemma or problem is the fourth phase of the PI model. Garrison and Anderson (2003, p. 60) suggest that the results from the resolution phase often "raise further questions and issues, triggering new cycles of inquiry, and, thereby, encouraging continuous learning." The application and resolution phase of the ITBL program involved the implementation and evaluation of the course redesign project. This phase is often overlooked in professional development programs. In many programs, faculty receive support for the design and development of their projects, but the implementation stage takes place after the program has been completed. Thus, faculty are left on their own to struggle through the initial implementation of their course redesign, and in most cases little or no evaluation is conducted to determine the effectiveness of the project from either a student or a faculty perspective.

To overcome these deficiencies, the ITBL cohort was maintained throughout this phase, and the participants intentionally engaged in the process of the scholarship of teaching and learning (SoTL). To facilitate this process, a discussion of the SoTL process was conducted in one of the early face-to-face ITBL cohort meetings. These conversations involved ITBL faculty mentors who had experience with the SoTL approach and thus could demonstrate their study processes and results. Faculty were encouraged to engage in the SoTL process from the outset of their ITBL projects. By applying for institutional ethics approval at the beginning of the course redesign process, project teams were able to collect data in the form of surveys, interviews, and focus groups with students, faculty, and teaching assistants who had been involved in past iterations of the course. Several projects also obtained data on student grades and withdrawal/dropout rates for comparison with the traditional sections. The collection and analysis of the data then allowed the project team to make informed course redesign decisions such as the proper selection and integration of face-to-face and online learning activities.

Although each course redesign project had its own specific SoTL needs and research study design, ethics approval was also obtained for the entire ITBL program to collect a common set of data for each of the project implementations. Analysis of the data was used to inform future offerings of the redesigned courses and to create an institutional course redesign inventory that could be used for academic program planning. Two sets of data collection techniques used included an end-of-semester student survey using the CoI questionnaire (Appendix D), described in Chapter 5, and a post-course interview with the faculty and teaching assistants responsible for the redesigned course.

The ITBL program was designed to help faculty define their course goals and expectations, redesign their learning activities and assessment assignments, adapt and develop online learning tools, evaluate course implementations, and disseminate results. This program supported the redesign of over 50 courses, and many of them significantly reduced or eliminated lectures entirely in favour of more engaged learning processes. Skibba and Widmer (2021) replicated our ITBL program at the University of Wisconsin—Madison, and their study findings indicate that a blended faculty Community of Inquiry can transform online teaching perceptions and practices.

Conclusion

There are those who predict the emergence of a blended campus for the post-COVID-19 higher education institution (Picciano, 2021). They indicate that during the pandemic many institutions adopted a mix of face-to-face and online delivery of courses and services, thus creating an opportunity for a more permanent shift to a blended university.

As emphasized in this chapter, Clark et al. (2021) argue that this will occur only through collaborative and visionary leadership. They recommend using the return-to-campus task forces convened during the pandemic to create a shared vision for a blended campus, align resources, and establish a road map to identify what the institution can do and where partnerships are needed. Sá and Serpa (2020) also describe how the pandemic might provide opportunities for innovative approaches to teaching in higher education, such as blended learning, but they indicate that the challenge will be for academic leaders to "stay the course" in order to sustain these types of transformation. In the final chapter, we provide concluding thoughts on future directions for a collaborative constructivist approach to blended learning in higher education.

Conclusion

To teach is to learn twice.

—(Joubert, 1842)

Garrison (2016, p. 113) reminds us that, despite the increasing prevalence of communication technologies, "thinking collaboratively must not be defined by the technology, regardless of how beneficial it is in connecting people." That is, digital technologies should not define how we approach thinking and learning. The nature and purpose of the collaboration will stimulate thinking and shape the discourse leading to meaningful construction and confirmation of knowledge. The great strength of blended approaches to thinking collaboratively is that they are not dependent on one mode of communication or technology.

Throughout this book, we have demonstrated the possibilities of a thoughtful blend of face-to-face and online synchronous and asynchronous learning opportunities. This approach integrates the lively give and take of face-to-face verbal discourse (complete with body language) and the reflective engagement made possible by asynchronous written communication. Advances in digital technologies should not necessarily be viewed as desirable replacements for learning in face-to-face environments. The option of face-to-face interaction should be considered carefully and not replaced simply because of technological advances and financial constraints. Technology does not replace teaching presence, whether it is in face-to-face or online learning environments.

We have also discussed in this book how there has been a shift from an individualistic, linear approach to a more collaborative, cyclical approach to learning (Kromydas, 2017), which from our perspective has been accelerated by the COVID-19 pandemic. As we indicated in the Introduction, a collaborative, cyclical approach to learning is closely aligned with Indigenous ways of knowing.

Indigenous Ways of Knowing

As cited in our Introduction, Wilson (2012) indicates that the ability to collaborate is linked to the origin of human intelligence and evolution. Humans have an innate ability to share their thoughts through communication that allows the group to accomplish more than the individual can alone. The era of COVID-19 has demonstrated to us that, when we collaborate at an international level, we can solve global problems. The hope is that we can now apply these global strategies of collaboration to other pressing issues, such as the climate crisis.

In the context of higher education, the historical ideal has been to learn in collaborative communities of inquiry, which can foster the growth and development of shared metacognition (Lipman, 1991). This has been demonstrated by Indigenous communities over time throughout the world. We would now like to summarize how our seven principles of blended learning align with Indigenous ways of knowing.

Our first principle involves designing for open communication and trust in order to create a blended learning community. This principle addresses the need to establish a social presence to support open communication and the development of cohesive group identity. The primary goal is to create a climate that encourages and supports open communication through a sense of belonging and trust. This principle aligns directly with the Canadian Inuit concept of *tunnganarniq*, which involves fostering a good spirit by being open, welcoming, and inclusive (Government of Nunavut, 2007). Storytelling is a common Indigenous practice to create such a learning environment. Everyone has stories to tell, and storytelling can contribute to key social presence elements such as inclusion, connection, and the beginning of a class community (Health Foundation, 2016). In addition, Blackfoot Elder Little Bear (2012) indicates that the power of storytelling is that, each time we tell or hear a story, we learn something new. It is an upward spiral of learning.

The second principle is designing for critical reflection and discourse to support inquiry. This principle focuses on cognitive presence, and we discussed the challenge of "pathological politeness" when trying to apply this principle in practice in regard to peer feedback. Garrison (2017, p. 53) documented how students often are unwilling to disagree with or challenge each other in a higher education course, especially in online discussion forums, since they do not want to offend or hurt anyone's feelings, a sense of "pathological politeness." To overcome this issue, the Lil'wat First Nation of Vancouver Island emphasizes the importance of *cwelelep* (Sanford et al., 2012). This concept recognizes the need sometimes to be in a place of dissonance and uncertainty so as to be open to new learning. In a broad sense, this concept is similar to Piaget's (1975) notion of cognitive dissonance, which Piaget suggested led to knowledge acquisition through assimilation to and accommodation with our existing mental frameworks.

Our third principle is the importance of establishing community and cohesion in a blended course. This principle is associated with social presence and focused on group identity and cohesion through open communication. For students to be socially present, they must have the opportunity to interact with each other. Again the challenge is that many students in higher education have limited experience and guidance with how to work collaboratively in a group. It is crucial that the teacher provide the students with guidance and opportunities to learn how to collaborate effectively in a group. We discussed Tuckman's (1965) five stages of group development, which in many ways align with the Indigenous Medicine Wheel that consists of four quadrants. Some teachers have begun to introduce this framework in their blended and online courses in order to emphasize multicultural ways of knowing and resilience in group settings (Bell, 2014).

The fourth principle is establishing the dynamics of inquiry in a blended course, which relate to the cognitive presence sphere of the CoI framework, derived from Garrison et al.'s (2000) PI model. Facilitation is necessary to set in motion and guide the dynamics of inquiry. In a blended environment, integrated face-to-face and online learning opportunities can allow for increased interaction, timely reflection, and continuous debate, all of which help to support the process of inquiry. As we discussed, the challenge for many of us in higher education is that we have been conditioned to focus on an individual, linear approach to learning and thus find it difficult to adapt to a cyclical and iterative approach to inquiry. We illustrated how the PI model aligns with the Anishinaabe Medicine Wheel framework for education (Bell, 2014). Both models consist of four interconnected quadrants that students move through in a cyclical nature. The key for us as educators is to demonstrate explicitly to our students the cyclical and interconnected nature of inquiry.

Our fifth principle involves sustaining respect and responsibility for collaboration. This principle is associated with social presence responsibilities. It focuses on sustaining a supportive environment and addressing issues that can undermine the group's trust and sense of belonging. Recall that social presence is concerned with open communication, group cohesion, and interpersonal relationships. The Canadian Inuit refer to an analogue of this principle as *inuuqatigiitsiarniq*, which involves respecting others, developing relationships, and caring for people (Government of Nunavut, 2007). The Inuit indicate that this is a lifelong disposition that needs to be reinforced throughout one's educational journey.

The sixth principle is about sustaining inquiry that moves to resolution and shared metacognitive development. The principle addresses issues of cognitive presence. It concerns scholarly leadership and is associated with critical discourse, reflection, and progression through the phases of practical inquiry. This principle involves the teacher and peers "nudging" fellow students forward in their academic studies (Thaler & Sunstein, 2008). This can be seen to aligns with the Lil'wat First Nation of Vancouver Island concept of *celhcelh*, in which people are responsible for their own and others learning, always seeking collaborative learning opportunities and support (Sanford et al., 2012).

Finally, our seventh principle ensures that assessment is aligned with learning outcomes and growth for all students in a blended course. In regard to this principle, we indicated that a report by the International Commission on the Futures of Education (2021) advocates that assessment needs to evolve from a mode of compliance to a process of shared goal setting, which leads to growth and development for all students. This approach to assessment can be seen as possessing an affinity with Indigenous perspectives. Claypool and Preston (2011) state that Euro-American-centric practices of assessment focus on written quizzes, tests, and exams, which primarily promote cognitive development via rational, linear, and accountable activities. They suggest that this approach to assessment is focused largely on meeting curricular outcomes, and it tends to neglect the physical, emotional, and spiritual domains of students. Marule (2012) suggests that effective assessment from an Indigenous perspective utilizes practices that include the cognitive domain but focus equally on physical, emotional, intellectual, and spiritual growth and development.

Conclusion

For a blended course, it is important to design and scaffold learning activities that support shared thinking and learning (shared metacognition) with an ethic of care (socio-emotional presence). Please keep in mind that the creation of a learning community takes time, and thus metacognitive awareness and patience are important.

Facilitation is most critical in the earliest stages of a blended course, and direct instruction becomes more important as the complexity and cognitive load of a task or an assignment increase. Our experience suggests that facilitation is necessary to set in motion the dynamics of inquiry, but direct instruction is required when techniques of facilitation do not move along the process of inquiry in a timely manner to the integration and resolution/application phases.

Remember that the teacher is the learning leader for a Community of Inquiry. Similar to a captain's responsibility for moving a ship forward, the teacher needs to "nudge" students to move beyond exploration to the integration and resolution phases of inquiry. As with facilitation, there is a delicate balance with direct instruction. Too much or too little direction from the teacher will affect adversely the engagement of students and their willingness to assume metacognitively teaching presence responsibilities.

In a blended Community of Inquiry, digital technologies can be used to create a triadic approach to assessment. Self-, peer, and teacher feedback techniques should be an integrated process rather than a series of isolated events in order to help students develop shared metacognitive awareness and strategies.

Finally, the CoI framework is available to support and sustain changes across multiple levels in education organizations. Engaging faculty in Communities of Inquiry that rest on collaborative processes not only supports changes to the student experience through course redesign but also offers a model of shared, collaborative, and collegial knowledge and skill development. The same process of leading collaboratively using a CoI approach can create an organizational culture in which leadership is a shared responsibility. We submit that collaborative leadership across all levels of an organization is key to the successful adoption of blended learning in higher education. This type of leadership engages individuals across an organization, engendering commitment and confidence in blended approaches to learning. It begins with creating blended faculty Communities of Inquiry in which faculty learn through experience the essence of collaborative inquiry and the shared leadership required to make it happen.

Appendix A
Blended Learning Design Process

Find a digital template that you can print or make a copy at https://tinyurl.com/blendedcoursetemplate.

Course/Learning Outcomes

What do you want your students to know when they have finished your course (e.g., key learning outcomes: knowledge, skills, and attitudes)?

- Example: Introduction to Teaching Course. Communicate effectively, using the language and concepts of teaching and learning.

Assessment Activities

How will you and your students know whether they have achieved these learning outcomes (e.g., opportunities for self-, peer, and instructor assessment)?

- Online quizzes—10%
- Journals—20%
- Clicker quizzes—10%
- Wiki summaries—10%
- Peer reviews—15%
- Portfolios—35%

Before a Synchronous Session

How will you help students to determine what prior knowledge and experience they have with the assessment activity?

- Assign a pre-class reading with an individual online quiz in Blackboard (four concept questions and one "What did you not understand?" question).

During a Synchronous Session

How will students synchronously interact and engage with the assessment activity?

- Use study groups to discuss the concept questions.
- Give a mini lecture to reinforce the concepts and diagnose student misconceptions.

After a Synchronous Session

What portion of this assessment activity will require "reflective time" for interaction and communication?

- An assigned study group will summarize the class discussion on the course wiki.
- Students can use these co-constructed summaries for their research projects and portfolios.

Tools

Which tools can be used to help organize, facilitate, and direct these assessment activities?

- Social bookmarking application
- Quiz tool in Blackboard
- Course wiki
- Peer review tool
- E-portfolio

Appendix B
Community of Inquiry: Teacher Self-Assessment and Exploration Tool

Find a digital template that you can print or make a copy at https://tinyurl.com/coiteacher.

Instructions: Read the behavioural indicator and give yourself a rating of (1) never, (2) rarely, (3) sometimes, (4) often, or (5) always. Record your evidence indicators or pedagogical practice to be explicit about how you work toward each indicator. Celebrate your success and note the CoI overlap and emotional presence/earning connection to build knowledge, reflect, and explore areas for growth.

Cognitive Presence

Triggering Event

Triggering events are dilemmas or problems that have practical resonance; they often include deeper questioning and generation of constructive ideas (Garrison, 2017).

CoI Survey Item	CoI Overlap	Emotional Presence/ Learning Connection
I pose problems and question prompts that increase student interest in course content.	Regulating learning	⇑ Engagement ⇑ Interest
I attempt to add content and discussion that trigger cohesive inquiry, open mindedness, and interest in deeper exploration.	Regulating learning	⇑ Curiosity ⇑ Interest

Exploration

Explore problems, link new and prior knowledge, and provide and deliberate possible contingencies and solutions.

I facilitate online discussions in a way that helps students to appreciate different perspectives.	Supporting discourse	⇑ Acceptance ⇑ Honouring diversity
I encourage exploration and motivation to explore content-related questions.	Supporting discourse	⇑ Curiosity ⇑ Interest
I create opportunities for students to combine information to explore questions raised in course activities.	Regulating learning	⇑ Curiosity

Integration

This involves a combination of critical, creative, and intuitive thinking that occurs as you construct meaning and experience deep learning.

I provide opportunities for reflection on course content and discussion that helps students to understand fundamental concepts.	Regulating learning	⇑ Metacognition
I select learning activities that help students to construct explanations/ solutions.	Regulating learning	⇑ Confidence ⇑ Pride
I provide a variety of information sources to help students explore problems posed in my course.	Regulating learning	⇑ Mastery ⇑ Curiosity

Resolution

Resolution can come from reducing complexity by constructing order or discovering a contextually specific solution to a defined problem.

I create course components to build conditions for students to describe ways to test and apply the knowledge learned.	Regulating learning	⇑ Pride ⇑ Confidence
I create opportunities for brainstorming and finding relevant information that helps students to seek resolution of content-related questions.	Regulating learning	⇑ Confidence ⇑ Pride ⇑ Self-directedness
I provide opportunities for students to develop solutions to relevant problems that can be applied in practice.	Regulating learning	⇑ Confidence
I create opportunities for reflection that help students to apply the knowledge created in my course to their work or other non-class-related activities.	Regulating learning	⇑ Metacognition

Social Presence

Affective (Personal) Expression

"A respectful and supportive climate is important to establish the emotional and intellectual conditions necessary for critical reflection and discourse" (Garrison 2017, p. 45).

I create opportunities for students to get to know their peers in this course in order to create a sense of belonging.	Setting climate	⇑ Belonging
I try to model online or web-based communication as an excellent medium for interaction.	Supporting discourse	⇑ Comfort ⇑ Confidence

Open Communication

"Open communication is built through a process of recognizing, complementing and responding to the questions and contributions of others, thereby . . . encouraging reflective participation and discourse" (Garrison, 2017, p. 46).

I work to ensure that students feel comfortable participating in course discussions.	Supporting discourse	⇑ Comfort ⇑ Risk-free expression
I create opportunities for students to develop comfort while interacting with other course participants.	Supporting discourse	⇑ Comfort ⇑ Interaction opportunities
I try to ensure that learners feel comfortable conversing online or in person in my course.	Setting climate	⇑ Comfort

Group Cohesion

Group cohesion in a Community of Inquiry is linked to shared goals and strong communication. The group will feel more cohesive if individuals extend purposeful efforts to demonstrate collaborative constructivist learning principles, including respect for diversity, inclusion, and belonging. Group cohesion is developed over time and leads to a collective identity.

I work to ensure that students feel comfortable disagreeing with other course participants while still maintaining a sense of trust.	Setting climate	⇑ Belonging
I work to ensure that students believe that other course participants acknowledge their points of view.	Setting climate	⇑ Honouring diversity ⇑ Acceptance ⇑ Belonging
I work to ensure that online or in-person discussions can help students to develop a sense of collaboration.	Setting climate	⇑ Shared metacognition ⇑ Belonging

Teaching Presence

Design and Organization

At the student level, it's about structuring, planning, and choosing what to add in terms of links and resources, materials that stimulate meaningful reflection; Garrison (2017) uses the phrase "broadening and channeling course content." He also discusses the idea of influencing content based upon evolving needs.

I provide clear instructions on how to participate in course learning activities, including explicit teaching about collaborative constructivist learning design.	Regulating learning	⇑ Comfort
I clearly communicate important course topics.	Regulating learning	⇓ Confusion
I clearly communicate important due dates/time frames for learning activities.	Setting climate	⇓ Hesitation

I clearly communicate important course goals, including explicit teaching about collaborative constructivist learning design and metacognitive goals.	Setting climate	↓ Hesitation

Facilitation

Facilitation is the central activity in an educational Community of Inquiry for developing worthwhile learning experiences as well as awareness and strategies (shared metacognition) through sustained reflection by and discourse among students and teacher. Facilitative actions, by both students and teacher, create the climate, support discourse, and monitor learning.

I am helpful in guiding the class toward understanding course topics in a way that helps students to clarify their thinking.	Regulating learning	↑ Metacognition
My actions reinforce the development of a sense of community among course participants.	Setting climate	↑ Belonging
I encourage course participants to explore new concepts in my course.	Regulating learning	↑ Curiosity
I help to identify areas of agreement and disagreement on course topics in a way that facilitates learning.	Supporting discourse	↑ Ambiguity ↑ Metacognition
I provide opportunities for students to take on the role of teacher.	Regulating learning	↑ Self-efficacy ↑ Confidence
I keep course participants engaged and participating in productive dialogue.	Supporting discourse	↑ Engagement ↓ Boredom

Direct Instruction

I provide feedback in a timely fashion.	Regulating learning	↑ Motivation

I provide feedback that helps students to understand strengths and weaknesses relative to the course goals and objectives.	Regulating learning	⇑ Self-efficacy
I help to focus discussion on relevant issues in a way that helps students to learn.	Setting climate	⇑ Engagement ⇑ Interest ⇑ Metacognition
I communicate that expressing emotion in relation to sharing ideas is acceptable in my course.	EP (cognitive presence)	⇑ Emotional literacy
In my role as teacher, I demonstrate (role-model) emotion in my presentations and/or when facilitating discussions, online or in person.	EP (teaching presence) Setting climate	⇑ Confidence
I acknowledge the emotions expressed by the students in my course.	EP (teaching presence)	⇑ Belonging ⇑ Trust
I find myself responding emotionally to ideas or learning activities in my course.	EP (cognitive presence)	⇑ Role model metacognition
I create space for students to feel comfortable expressing emotions through the online medium or in the in-person classroom.	EP (social presence)	⇑ Comfort
I create space to ensure that emotions are expressed, online or in person, among the students in my course.	EP (social presence)	⇑ Metacognition ⇑ Trust

Appendix C
Community of Inquiry: Student Self-Assessment and Exploration Tool

Find a digital template that you can print or make a copy at https://tinyurl.com/coistudent.

Welcome to our learning community. This course is built with the Community of Inquiry (CoI) theoretical framework. A large part of the model is based upon the belief that we all have shared responsibility to contribute to teaching and learning. You can do this by building your skills in three key areas: supporting the discourse, setting the climate, and self- and co-regulation of learning. This self-assessment tool is built to help you make practical connections to the CoI framework. Embedded throughout the tool are links to emotional presence and affective learning outcomes through attention to increasing feelings of engagement, curiosity, belonging, pride, gratitude, and confidence regulating or reducing feelings of discomfort and hesitation. Consider this tool both an advanced organizer and an in situ reflection tool.

Instructions: Read the behavioural indicator in the first column and give yourself a rating of (1) never, (2) rarely, (3) sometimes, (4) often, or (5) always at the beginning, the midpoint, and the end of the course. Celebrate your success and use the second and third columns to develop a deeper understanding of the learning theory that is the foundation of CoI learning. Reflect and document growth and development throughout the course.

Cognitive Presence

Triggering Event

Triggering events are dilemmas or problems that have practical resonance. They often include deeper questioning and generation of constructive ideas (Garrison, 2017).

CoI Survey Item	CoI Overlap	Emotional Presence/ Learning Connection
I pose problems and questions that help to engage and increase my own and my peers' interest in the course concepts.	Regulating learning	Increase engagement Increase interest
I attempt to add content and discussion that triggers cohesive inquiry, open mindedness, and interest in deeper exploration.	Regulating learning	Increase curiosity Increase interest

Exploration

This involves exploring problems, linking new and prior knowledge, and providing and deliberating possible contingencies and solutions.

CoI Survey Item	CoI Overlap	Emotional Presence/ Learning Connection
I am motivated to explore content-related questions, and I encourage my peers to explore these questions.	Supporting discourse	Increase curiosity Increase interest Increase belonging/ inclusion Increase self-regulation
I participate in discussions in a way that helps my peers to appreciate different perspectives and express emotions in relation to content.	Supporting discourse	Increase acceptance Honour diversity Emotional literacy

I create opportunities for collective brainstorming that help me and my peers to explore content dilemmas and related questions.	Regulating learning	Increase confidence Increase pride Increase self-directedness
I provide a variety of information sources (literature and links) to help me and my peers think collaboratively to explore problems.	Regulating learning	Promote mastery Increase curiosity

Integration

In the integration phase, you might feel dissonance as you appraise the collective dialogue about personal beliefs, experiences, and practical examples related to course content. Integration involves a combination of critical, creative, and intuitive thinking that occurs as you construct meaning and experience deep learning.

I utilize opportunities for reflection on course content and discussion that help me and my peers to connect ideas to understand fundamental course concepts.	Supporting discourse	Increase metacognitive awareness Increase critical thinking
I create opportunities for me and my peers to combine information to explore questions raised in course activities by using a combination of reflection, discourse, and reflexivity.	Regulating learning	Generate curiosity Increase reflection Increase reflexivity
I feel confident to apply learning strategies that help me and my peers to examine rationally assumptions, ideas, and evidence to confirm understanding.	Regulating learning	Increase confidence Increase pride Promote co-regulation Increase metacognition

Resolution

Resolution can come from reducing complexity by constructing order or discovering a contextually specific solution to a defined problem.

I use the discussion board to discuss/ describe how I apply knowledge from the course.	Regulating learning	Increase metacognition
I have developed contextually specific solutions to course problems.	Regulating learning	Increase pride Increase confidence
I can directly apply the knowledge created in this course to my everyday life and/or work.	Regulating learning	Increase confidence Increase lifelong learning disposition

Teaching Presence

Design and Organization

At the student level, this is about structuring, planning, and choosing what to add in terms of links, resources, and materials that stimulate meaningful reflection. Garrison (2017) uses the phrase "broadening and channeling course content." He also discusses the idea of influencing content based upon evolving needs.

I actively engage to meet important due dates/time frames for the course activities.	Setting/ cultivating climate	Decrease hesitation Self-regulation and planning
I participate in broadening and channelling course content to aid collective understanding.	Supporting discourse	Reduce confusion Promote shared metacognition
I direct attention and effort to participate in course learning activities, based upon the evolving needs of our learning community.	Regulating learning	Increase comfort

Facilitation

Facilitation is the central activity in an educational Community of Inquiry for developing worthwhile learning experiences as well as awareness and strategies (shared metacognition) through sustained reflection and discourse among the students and the teacher. Facilitative actions by both the students and the teacher create the climate, support discourse, and monitor learning.

I help to identify areas of agreement and disagreement on course topics with my peers in a way that nurtures a shared learning experience.	Supporting discourse	Reduce ambiguity Increase metacognition Increase task motivation
My actions reinforce and develop responsibility for the collaborative climate and sense of community.	Setting and cultivating climate	Increase belonging Increase co-regulation
I encourage my peers to explore new concepts in this course by showing appreciation of and gratitude for well-reasoned responses.	Regulating learning	Increase curiosity
I feel confident taking on the role of teacher for my peers when the opportunity arises.	Regulating learning	Increase self-efficacy Increase confidence
I keep my peers engaged and participating in productive dialogue in this course.	Supporting discourse	Increase engagement Decrease boredom Increase co-regulation
I am helpful in guiding our course discussions toward understanding key concepts in a way that helps us all to clarify our thinking.	Regulating learning	Increase metacognitive monitoring

Direct Instruction

Direct instruction is not about lecturing; it is about scholarly and pedagogical leadership. Direct instruction is an essential ingredient of any formal educational experience in order to help students learn how to take responsibility collaboratively to monitor and manage their learning (shared metacognition).

I help to focus our course discussions on relevant issues in a way that leads to deeper exploration.	Setting and cultivating climate	Increase engagement Increase interest Increase metacognition
I contribute to our course discussions in a timely fashion.	Regulating learning	Increase motivation
I add to course discussions and activities in a way that connects outside resources and personal examples.	Regulating learning	Increase self-efficacy

Social Presence

Affective (Personal) Expression

"A respectful and supportive climate is important to establish the emotional and intellectual conditions necessary for critical reflection and discourse" (Garrison, 2017, p. 45).

I ask questions to get to know my peers in order to create a sense of belonging.	Setting and cultivating climate	Promote belonging
I create opportunities to let my peers get to know me on a personal level.	Setting and cultivating climate	Promote belonging Extend trust
I approach discussion in a way that models respectful and supportive interaction.	Supporting discourse	Increase comfort Increase confidence Promote inclusion

Open Communication

"Open communication is built through a process of recognizing, complementing, and responding to the questions and contributions of others, thereby ... encouraging reflective participation and discourse" (Garrison, 2017, p. 46).

I try to ensure that my peers feel comfortable conversing about related topics in this course.	Setting and cultivating climate	Increase comfort
I work to ensure that my peers feel that our learning community is a safe space for emotional expression and respectful participation.	Supporting discourse	Increase comfort Promote risk-free expression Increase trust

Group Cohesion

I work to ensure that my peers feel comfortable disagreeing with each other while still maintaining a sense of trust.	Setting and cultivating climate	Promote belonging
I work to ensure that my peers believe that their points of view are acknowledged before adding my own understanding.	Setting and cultivating climate	Honour diversity Extend acceptance Emotional resonance
I participate in or lead learning activities that help to develop a sense of collaboration.	Setting and cultivating climate	Shared metacognition Belonging Sustained motivation

Appendix D
Community of Inquiry Survey Instrument

Find a digital template that you can print or make a copy at https://coi.athabascau.ca/coi-model/coi-survey/.

Teaching Presence

Design and Organization
1. The instructor clearly communicated important course topics.
2. The instructor clearly communicated important course goals.
3. The instructor provided clear instructions on how to participate in course learning activities.
4. The instructor clearly communicated important due dates/time frames for learning activities.

Facilitation
5. The instructor was helpful in identifying areas of agreement and disagreement on course topics that helped me to learn.
6. The instructor was helpful in guiding the class toward understanding course topics in a way that helped me to clarify my thinking.

7. The instructor helped to keep course participants engaged and participating in productive dialogue.
8. The instructor helped to keep the course participants on task in a way that helped me to learn.
9. The instructor encouraged course participants to explore new concepts in this course.
10. Instructor actions reinforced the development of a sense of community among course participants.

Direct Instruction

11. The instructor helped to focus discussion on relevant issues in a way that helped me to learn.
12. The instructor provided feedback that helped me to understand my strengths and weaknesses relative to the course's goals and objectives.
13. The instructor provided feedback in a timely fashion.

Social Presence

Affective Expression

14. Getting to know other course participants gave me a sense of belonging in the course.
15. I was able to form distinct impressions of some course participants.
16. Online or web-based communication is an excellent medium for social interaction.

Open Communication

17. I felt comfortable conversing through the online medium.
18. I felt comfortable participating in the course discussions.
19. I felt comfortable interacting with other course participants.

Group Cohesion

20. I felt comfortable disagreeing with other course participants while still maintaining a sense of trust.
21. I thought that my point of view was acknowledged by other course participants.
22. Online discussions helped me to develop a sense of collaboration.

Cognitive Presence

Triggering Event

23. Problems posed increased my interest in course issues.
24. Course activities piqued my curiosity.
25. I felt motivated to explore content-related questions.

Exploration

26. I utilized a variety of information sources to explore problems posed in this course.
27. Brainstorming and finding relevant information helped me to resolve content-related questions.
28. Online discussions were valuable in helping me to appreciate different perspectives.

Integration

29. Combining new information helped me to answer questions raised in course activities.
30. Learning activities helped me to construct explanations/ solutions.
31. Reflection on course content and discussions helped me to understand fundamental concepts in this class.

Resolution

32. I can describe ways to test and apply the knowledge created in this course.

33. I have developed solutions to course problems that can be applied in practice.
34. I can apply the knowledge created in this course to my work or other non-class-related activities.

Likert-Type Scale

1 = strongly disagree, 2 = disagree, 3 = neutral, 4 = agree, 5 = strongly agree

Appendix E
Shared Metacognition Questionnaire

When I am engaged in the learning process as an individual:
SELF-REGULATION

I1: I am aware of my effort.

I2: I am aware of my thinking.

I3: I know my level of motivation.

I4: I question my thoughts.

I5: I make judgments about the difficulty of a problem.

I6: I am aware of my existing knowledge.

I7: I assess my understanding.

I8: I change my strategy when I need to.

I9: I am aware of my level of learning.

I10: I search for new strategies when needed.

I11: I apply strategies.

I12: I assess how I approach the problem.

I13: I assess my strategies.

When I am engaged in the learning process as a member of a group:
CO-REGULATION

G1: I pay attention to the ideas of others.

G2: I listen to the comments of others.

G3: I consider the feedback of others.

G4: I reflect on the comments of others.

G5: I observe the strategies of others.

G6: I observe how others are doing.

G7: I look for confirmation of my understanding from others.

G8: I request information from others.

G9: I respond to the contributions that others make.

G10: I challenge the strategies of others.

G11: I challenge the perspectives of others.

G12: I help the learning of others.

G13: I monitor the learning of others.

Likert-Type Scale

1 = strongly disagree, 2 = disagree, 3 = neutral, 4 = agree, 5 = strongly agree

References

Absolon, K. (2019). Indigenous wholistic theory: A knowledge set for practice. *First Peoples Child & Family Review, 14*(1), 22–42.

Ahrensmeier, D., Donev, J. M. K. C., Hicks, R. B., Louro, A. A., Sangalli, L., Stafford, R. B., & Thompson, R. I. (2009). Labatorials at the University of Calgary: In pursuit of effective small group instruction within large registration physics service courses. *Physics in Canada, 65*(4), 214–216.

Akyol, Z., & Garrison, D. R. (2008). The development of a community of inquiry over time in an online course: Understanding the progression and integration of social, cognitive and teaching presence. *Journal of Asynchronous Learning Networks, 12*(3), 3–22.

Alberta Regional Consortia. (2022). Empowering the spirit: Sharing through story. https://empoweringthespirit.ca/sharing-through-story/

The Alberta Teachers' Association. (2022). Professional growth plans. https://www.teachers.ab.ca/For%20Members/ProfessionalGrowth/Pages/Teacher%20Professional%20Growth%20Plans.aspx

Ali, D. (2017). Safe spaces and brave spaces: Historical context and recommendations for student affairs professionals. *NASPA Policy and Practice Series.* https://www.naspa.org/images/uploads/main/Policy_and_Practice_No_2_Safe_Brave_Spaces.pdf

Alton-Lee, A. (2003). *Quality teaching for diverse students in schooling: Best evidence synthesis June 2003.* Wellington, NZ: Ministry of Education.

Angelo, T. A., & Cross, K. P. (1993). *Classroom assessment techniques: A handbook for college teachers* (2nd ed.). Jossey-Bass.

Arbaugh, J. B. (2008). Does the community of inquiry framework predict outcomes in online MBA courses? *International Review of Research in Open and Distance Learning, 9*, 1–21.

Arbaugh, J. B., Cleveland-Innes, M., Diaz, S. R., Garrison, D. R., Ice, P., Richardson, J. C., & Swan, K. P. (2008). Developing a Community of Inquiry instrument: Testing a measure of the community of inquiry framework using a multi-institutional sample. *The Internet and Higher Education, 11*(3–4), 133–136.

Asad, K. (2013). Understanding the pareto principle (the 80/20 rule). *Better Explained.* https://betterexplained.com/articles/understanding-the-pareto-principle-the-8020-rule/

Austen Kay, A. (2021, August 26). How online mindfulness training can help students thrive during the pandemic. *The Conversation.* https://theconversation.com/how-online-mindfulness-training-can-help-students-thrive-during-the-pandemic-166264

Ausubel, D. P. (1968). *Educational psychology: A cognitive view.* Holt, Rinehart & Winston.

Bambino, D. (2002). Critical friends. *Redesigning Professional Development, 59*(6), 25–27. https://www.ascd.org/el/articles/critical-friends

Bartlett, C., Marshall, M., & Marshall, A. (2012). Two-eyed seeing and other lessons learned within a co-learning journey of bringing together Indigenous and mainstream knowledges and ways of knowing. *Journal of Environmental Studies and Sciences, 2*(10), 331–340.

Bashovski, M. (2021, September 28). Building classroom community, even when we're all alone. *Hybrid Pedagogy.* https://hybridpedagogy.org/building-classroom-community/

Bell, N. (2014). Teaching by the medicine wheel: An Anishinaabe framework for Indigenous education. *EdCan Network.* https://www.edcan.ca/articles/teaching-by-the-medicine-wheel/

Biggs, J. (1996). Enhancing teaching through constructive alignment. *Higher Education, 32*, 347–364. https://doi.org/10.1007/BF00138871

Biggs, J. (1998). Assumptions underlying new approaches to assessment. In P. Stimson & P. Morris (Eds), *Curriculum and assessment in Hong Kong: Two components, one system* (pp. 351–384). Open University of Hong Kong Press.

Bjerke, M. B., & Renger, R. (2017). Being smart about writing SMART objectives. *Evaluation and Program Planning, 61*, 125–127. https://doi.org/10.1016/j.evalprogplan.2016.12.009

Blackboard. (2022). *Blackboard learning management system.* https://www.blackboard.com/

Blogger. (2022). *Blogger.* https://www.blogger.com/

Bloom, B. S., Englehart, M.D., Furst, E.J., Hill, W.H., & Krathwohl, D.R.(1956). *Taxonomy of educational objectives: Handbook 1: Cognitive domain.* David McKay.

Boelens, R., De Wever, B., & Voet, M. (2017). Four key challenges to the design of blended learning: A systematic literature review. *Educational Research Review, 22*, 1–18. https://doi.org/10.1016/j.edurev.2017.06.001

Bonk, C., Kim, K., & Zeng, X. (2004). Future directions of blended learning in higher education and workplace learning settings. In C. J. Bonk, & C. R. Graham (Eds.), *Handbook of blended learning: Global perspectives, local designs* (pp. 550–568). John Wiley & Sons.

Borup, J., West, R. E., & Thomas, R. (2015). The impact of text versus video communication on instructor feedback in blended courses. *Educational Technology Research and Development, 63*(2), 161–184. https://doi.org/10.1007/s11423-015-9367-8

Boud, D. (2000). Sustainable assessment: Rethinking assessment for the learning society. *Studies in Continuing Education, 22*(2), 151–167. http://www.education.uts.edu.au/ostaff/staff/publications/db_28_sce_00.pdf

Bozkurt, A. (2019). From distance education to open and distance learning: A holistic evaluation of history, definitions, and theories. In S. Sisman-Ugur & G. Kurubacak (Eds.), *Handbook of research on learning in the age of transhumanism* (pp. 252–273). IGI Global. https://doi.org/10.4018/978-1-5225-8431-5.ch016

Brame, C. (2013). Just-in-time teaching (JiTT). *Center for Teaching, Vanderbilt University.* https://cft.vanderbilt.edu/guides-sub-pages/just-in-time-teaching-jitt/

Brigham Young University. (2022). Concept mapping. https://ctl.byu.edu/tip/concept-mapping

Brown, C., Datt, A., Forbes, D., Gedera, D., & Hartnett, M. (2021). *Report: University students online learning experiences in COVID-times.* https://studentonlinelearningexperiences.wordpress.com/

Brown, J., & Isaacs, D. (2005). *The world café: Shaping our futures through conversations that matter*. Berrett-Koehler Publishers.

Brown, M. (2021, October 19). Integrative leadership: A necessary ingredient for Dx. *EDUCAUSE Review*, 40–43. https://er.educause.edu/blogs/2020/9/integrative-leadership-a-necessary-ingredient-for-dx

Brown, S. (2004). Assessment for learning. *Learning and Teaching in Higher Education*, *1*, 81–89. https://eprints.glos.ac.uk/3607/1/

Burns, R. (1785). To a mouse. *Poetry Foundation*. https://www.poetryfoundation.org/poems/43816/to-a-mouse-56d222ab36e33

Cajete, G. (1994). *Look to the mountain: An ecology of Indigenous education*. Kivaki Press.

Caldwell, J. (2021, May 11). Effectively moving away from traditional proctored exams in first-year physics courses. *BC Campus News*. https://bccampus.ca/2021/05/11/effectively-moving-away-from-traditional-proctored-exams-in-first-year-physics-courses/

Canvas. (2022). *Canvas learning management system*. https://www.instructure.com/canvas

Carnegie Mellon University. (2022). Sample group project tools. https://www.cmu.edu/teaching/designteach/teach/instructionalstrategies/groupprojects/tools/index.html

Carriere, J. (2010). Editorial: Gathering, sharing and documenting the wisdom within and across our communities and academic circles. *First Peoples Child & Family Review*, *5*(1), 5–7.

Chang, Y., & Brickman, P. (2018). When group work doesn't work: Insights from students. *CBE Life Sciences Education*, *17*(3), ar42. https://doi.org/10.1187/cbe.17-09-0199

Chiang, F.-K., & Wu, Z. (2021). Flipping a classroom with a three-stage collaborative instructional model (3-CI) for graduate students. *Australasian Journal of Educational Technology*, *37*(4), 51–67. https://doi.org/10.14742/ajet.6330

Chick, N. (2013). Metacognition. *Center for Teaching, Vanderbilt University*. https://cft.vanderbilt.edu/guides-sub-pages/metacognition/

Chiroma, J. A., Meda, L., & Waghid, Z. (2021). Examining emergency remote teaching using the community of inquiry framework: Lecturer experiences in a Kenyan university. *International Journal of Information and*

Communication Technology Education (IJICTE), 17(4), 1–16. https://doi
.org/10.4018/IJICTE.20211001.0a17

Clark, C., Wittmayer, A., Noone, D., & Selingo, J. J. (2021). The hybrid
campus. *Deloitte Insights*. https://www2.deloitte.com/us/en/insights/
industry/public-sector/post-pandemic-hybrid-learning.html

Clase, K. L., Grundlach, E., & Pelaez, N. J. (2010). Calibrated peer
review for computer-assisted learning for biological research
competencies. *Biochemistry and Molecular Biology Education,
38*(5), 290–295.

Claypool, T. R., & Preston, J. P. (2011). Redefining learning and assessment
practices impacting Aboriginal students: Considering Aboriginal priorities
via Aboriginal and Western worldviews. *Education, 17*(3), 84–95. https://
doi.org/10.1037/e683152011-019

Cleveland-Innes, M., Garrison, R., & Kinsel, E. (2007). Role adjustment for
learners in an online community of inquiry: Identifying the challenges of
incoming online learners. *International Journal of Web-Based Learning and
Teaching Technologies, 2*(1), 1–16.

Cleveland-Innes, M., & Wilton, D. (2018). Guide to blended learning.
Commonwealth of Learning. http://oasis.col.org/handle/11599/3095

Cmap. (2022). *CmapTools.* https://cmap.ihmc.us/cmaptools/

Coggle. (2022). *Coggle application.* https://coggle.it/

Conrad, D., & Openo, J. (2018). *Assessment strategies for online learning.*
Athabasca University Press. https://www.aupress.ca/books/120279
-assessment-strategies-for-online-learning/

Costa, A. L., & Kalick, B. (1993). Through the lens of a critical friend.
Educational Leadership, 51(2), 49–51.

Crow, J., & Murray, J.-A. (2020). Online distance learning in biomedical
sciences: Community, belonging and presence. In P. Rea (Ed.), *Biomedical
visualisation: Advances in experimental medicine and biology* (Vol. 1235).
Springer. https://doi.org/10.1007/978-3-030-37639-0_10.

Csíkszentmihályi, M. (1997). *Creativity: Flow and the psychology of discovery
and invention.* HarperPerennial.

Cuesta Medina, L. (2018). Blended learning: Deficits and prospects in higher
education. *Australasian Journal of Educational Technology, 34*(1), 42–56.
https://doi.org/10.14742/ajet.3100

Dennen, V. P. (2005). From message posting to learning dialogues: Factors affecting learner participation in asynchronous discussion. *Distance Education, 26*(1), 127–148.

deNoyelles, A., Zydney, J. M., & Chen, B. (2014). Strategies for creating a community of inquiry through online asynchronous discussions. *Journal of Online Learning and Teaching, 10*(1), 153–166. https://jolt.merlot.org/vol10no1/denoyelles_0314.pdf

Desire2Learn. (2022). *Brightspace learning management system.* https://www.d2l.com/

Dewey, J. (1933). *How we think.* Heath.

Dweck, C. S. (2006). *Mindset: The new psychology of success.* Random House.

Entwistle, N. (2003). Concepts and conceptual frameworks underpinning the ETL project. *Enhancing Teaching-Learning Environments in Undergraduate Courses Project, Higher and Community Education, School of Education, University of Edinburgh.* https://www.etl.tla.ed.ac.uk/docs/ETLreport3.pdf

Eom, S. (2006). The role of instructors as a determinant of students' satisfaction in university online education. In R. Koper (Ed.), *Proceedings of the Sixth IEEE International Conference on Advanced Learning Technologies* (pp. 985–988). IEEE Computer Society.

Eom, S. B., & Arbaugh, J. B. (Eds.). (2011). *Student satisfaction and learning outcomes in e-learning: An introduction to empirical research.* Information Science.

Fernandez, A. A., & Shaw, G. P. (2020). Academic leadership in a time of crisis: The coronavirus and COVID-19. *Journal of Leadership Studies, 14*(1), 39–45.

Flipgrid. (2022). *Flipgrid video discussion application.* https://info.flipgrid.com/

Freire, P. (2018). *Pedagogy of the oppressed: 50th anniversary edition.* Bloomsbury Academic.

Garrison, D. R. (2006). Online collaboration principles. *Online Learning Journal, 10*(1), 25–34. https://olj.onlinelearningconsortium.org/index.php/olj/article/view/1768

Garrison, D. R. (2009). Communities of inquiry in online learning. In P. L. Rogers, G. A. Berg, J. V. Boettcher, C. Howard, L. Justice, & K. D. Schenk (Eds.), *Encyclopedia of distance learning* (2nd ed., pp. 352–355). IGI Global.

Garrison, D. R. (2016). *Thinking collaboratively: Learning in a community of inquiry*. Routledge, Taylor & Francis.

Garrison, D. R. (2017). *E-learning in the 21st century: A community of inquiry framework for research and practice* (3rd ed.). Routledge, Taylor & Francis.

Garrison, D. R. (2018). Shared metacognition. *Community of Inquiry Blog*. http://www.thecommunityofinquiry.org/editorial16

Garrison, D. R. (2019). Implementing shared metacognition. *Community of Inquiry Blog*. http://www.thecommunityofinquiry.org/editorial19

Garrison, D. R., & Akyol, Z. (2015a). Toward the development of a metacognition construct for the community of inquiry framework. *Internet and Higher Education, 24*, 66–71. https://doi.org/10.1016/j.iheduc.2014.10.001

Garrison, D. R., & Akyol, Z. (2015b). Corrigendum to 'Toward the development of a metacognition construct for communities of inquiry.' *Internet and Higher Education, 26*, 56. https://doi.org/10.1016/j.iheduc.2014.10.001

Garrison, D. R., & Anderson, T. (2003). *E-learning in the 21st century: A framework for research and practice*. Routledge/Falmer.

Garrison, D. R., Anderson, T., & Archer, W. (2000). Critical inquiry in a text-based environment: Computer conferencing in higher education model. *The Internet and Higher Education, 2*(2–3), 87–105.

Garrison, D. R., Anderson, T., & Archer, W. (2001). Critical thinking, cognitive presence, and computer conferencing in distance education. *American Journal of Distance Education, 15*, 7–23. http://dx.doi.org/10.1080/08923640109527071

Garrison, D. R., & Cleveland-Innes, M. (2005). Facilitating cognitive presence in online learning: Interaction is not enough. *American Journal of Distance Education, 19*, 133–148. http://dx.doi.org/10.1207/s15389286ajde1903_2

Garrison, D. R., Cleveland-Innes, M., & Vaughan, N. D. (2022). Community of inquiry survey. *Community of Inquiry*. https://coi.athabascau.ca/coi-model/coi-survey/

Garrison, D. R., & Kanuka, H. (2004). Blended learning: Uncovering its transformative potential in higher education. *The Internet and Higher Education, 7*(2), 95–105.

Garrison, D. R., & Vaughan, N. D. (2008). *Blended learning in higher education*. Jossey-Bass.

Gierdowsk, D. C., Brooks, D. C., & Galanek, J. (2020). Supporting the whole student. *EDUCAUSE*. https://www.educause.edu/ecar/research-publications/student-technology-report-supporting-the-whole-student/2020/technology-use-and-environmental-preferences

Gooblar, D. (2021, March 24). Our slimmed-down pandemic pedagogy. *The Chronicle of Higher Education*. https://www.chronicle.com/article/our-slimmed-down-pandemic-pedagogy

Google. (2022a). *Google docs*. https://docs.google.com/

Google. (2022b). *Google forms*. https://www.google.ca/forms/about/

Google. (2022c). *Google jamboard*. https://jamboard.google.com/

Google. (2022d). *Google meet video conferencing application*. https://meet.google.com/

Google. (2022e). *Google sites*. https://sites.google.com/

Google. (2022f). *Google slides presentation application*. https://www.google.ca/slides/about/

Google. (2022g). *Google sheets*. https://www.google.ca/sheets/about/

Gordon, N. (2021). A permanent pivot to online learning, or will universities bounce back to normal? *Academia: Letters*. https://www.academia.edu/50331191/A_permanent_Pivot_to_online_learning_or_will_universities_bounce_back_to_normal

Government of Nunavut. (2007). Inuit *qaujimajatuqangit* education framework. https://www.gov.nu.ca/sites/default/files/files/Inuit%20Qaujimajatuqangit%20ENG.pdf

Government of Ontario. (2016). The learning conversations protocol. http://www.edu.gov.on.ca/eng/literacynumeracy/inspire/research/learning_conversations.pdf

Graham, C. R. (2019). Current research in blended learning. In M. G. Moore & W. C. Diehl (Eds.), *Handbook of distance education* (4th ed., pp. 173–188). Routledge.

Gurr, D., Drysdale, L., & Mulford, B. (2006). School leadership and management. *Models of Successful Principal Leadership, 26*(4), 371–395.

Hattie, J. (2009). *Visible learning: A synthesis of over 800 meta-analyses relating to achievement*. Routledge.

Hattie, J., & Yates, G. C. R. (2014). *Visible learning and the science of how we learn*. Routledge.

The Health Foundation. (2016). The power of storytelling. https://www
.health.org.uk/newsletter-feature/power-of-storytelling

Hedberg, J., & Corrent-Agostinho, S. (1999). Creating a postgraduate
virtual community: Assessment drives learning. In B. Collis & R. Oliver
(Eds.), *Proceedings of World Conference on Educational Multimedia,
Hypermedia and Telecommunications* (pp. 1093–1098). Association for the
Advancement of Computers in Education. http://www.editlib.org/p/7040

Hesterman, S. (2016). The digital handshake: A group contract for authentic
elearning in higher education. *Journal of University Teaching and Learning
Practice, 13*(3), 1–24.

Hite, S. (2020, May 20). How the world café model can enhance online
discussion. *Education Week.* https://www.edweek.org/education/
opinion-how-the-world-cafe-model-can-enhance-online-discussion/
2020/05

Houle, C. O. (1954). The evening college. *The Journal of Higher Education,
25*(7), 362–399.

Hyper Island. (2022). *IDOARRT meeting design.* https://toolbox.hyperisland
.com/idoarrt-meeting-design

International Commission on the Futures of Education. (2021). Reimagining
our futures together: A new social contract for education. *UNESCO.* https:
//unesdoc.unesco.org/ark:/48223/pf0000379707

Irvine, V. (2020). The landscape of merging modalities. *EDUCAUSE Review, 4,*
40–58. https://er.educause.edu/articles/2020/10/the-landscape-of
-merging-modalities

Iseke, J. M. (2010). Importance of Métis ways of knowing in healing
communities. *Canadian Journal of Native Education, 33*(1), 83–97.

Johnson, E. (2021, July 13). Digital learning is real-world learning. That's why
blended on-campus and online study is best. *The Conversation.* https://
theconversation.com/digital-learning-is-real-world-learning-thats-why
-blended-on-campus-and-online-study-is-best-163002

Johnson, N. (2019). *National survey of online and digital learning: 2019 national
report.* http://www.cdlra-acrfl.ca/wp-content/uploads/2020/07/2019
_national_en.pdf

Jooston, T., & Weber, N. (2021). Planning for a blended future: A research-
driven guide for educators. *Every Learner Everywhere.* https://www
.everylearnereverywhere.org/resources/planning-for-a-blended-future/

Joubert, J. (1842). *Pensees.* http://www.doyletics.com/art/notebook.htm

Kalman, C., La Braca, F., & Sobhanzadeh, M. (2020). Comparison of labatorials and traditional physics labs. *2020 American Society for Engineering Education Virtual Annual Conference.*

Kantor, B. (2018). The RACI matrix: Your blueprint for project success. *CIO.* https://www.cio.com/article/2395825/project-management-how-to-design -a-successful-raci-project-plan.html

Kent, S. (2016). Threshold concepts. *University of Calgary, Taylor Institute of Teaching and Learning.* https://taylorinstitute.ucalgary.ca/sites/default/ files/TI%20Guides/Threshold_Concepts_Guide.pdf

Kintu, M. J., Zhu, C., & Kagambe, E. (2017). Blended learning effectiveness: The relationship between student characteristics, design features and outcomes. *International Journal of Educational Technology in Higher Education, 14*(7), 1–20. https://doi.org/10.1186/s41239-017-0043-4

Knowles, M. S. (1986). *Using learning contracts.* Jossey-Bass.

Kritik. (2022). *Kritik: Peer assessment platform.* https://www.kritik.io/

Kromydas, T. (2017). Rethinking higher education and its relationship with social inequalities: Past knowledge, present state and future potential. *Palgrave Commun, 3*(1), 1–12. https://www.nature.com/articles/s41599-017 -0001-8#citeas

Lambrev, V. S., & Cruz, B. C. (2021). Becoming scholarly practitioners: Creating community in online professional doctoral education. *Distance Education, 42*(2), 561–581. https://doi.org/10.1080/01587919.2021 .1986374

LearnAlberta. (2008). Assessment in mathematics. https://www.learnalberta .ca/content/mewa/html/assessment/types.html

Lipman, M. (1991). *Thinking in education.* Cambridge University Press.

Littky, D., & Grabelle, S. (2004). *The big picture: Education is everyone's business.* Association for Supervision and Curriculum Development.

Little Bear, L. (2012). Traditional knowledge and humanities: A perspective by a Blackfoot. *Journal of Chinese Philosophy, 39*(4), 518–527. https:// onlinelibrary.wiley.com/doi/abs/10.1111/j.1540-6253.2012.01742.x

Loureiro, M. J., Pombo, L., & Moreira, A. (2012). The quality of peer assessment in a wiki-based online context: A qualitative study. *Educational Media International, 49*(2), 139–149. https://doi.org/10.1080/09523987 .2012.703426

Lucidspark. (2022). *Lucidspark virtual whiteboard.* https://lucidspark.com/

Lyryx. (2022). *Lyryx learning system.* https://lyryx.com/

Manitoba Education. (2006). Rethinking classroom assessment with purpose in mind. *Government of Manitoba.* https://digitalcollection.gov.mb.ca/awweb/pdfopener?smd=1&did=12503&md=1

Marton, F., & Saljo, R. (1984). Approaches to learning. In F. Marton, D. Hounsell, & N. Entwistle (Eds.), *The Experience of Learning* (pp. 39–58). Scottish Academic Press.

Marule, T. O. (2012). Niitsitapi relational and experiential theories in education. *Canadian Journal of Native Education, 35*(1), 131–143.

Menti. (2022). *Mentimeter.* https://www.menti.com/

Meyer, J., & Land, R. (2005). Threshold concepts and troublesome knowledge: Epistemological considerations and a conceptual framework for teaching and learning. *Higher Education, 49,* 373–388.

Microsoft. (2022). *Microsoft PowerPoint presentation software.* https://www.microsoft.com/en-us/microsoft-365/powerpoint

Mitchell, L., Campbell, C., Rigby, R., & Williams, L. T. (2021). Giving students an eDGE: Focusing on e-portfolios for graduate employability. *The Journal of Teaching and Learning for Graduate Employability, 12*(2), 316–331. https://ojs.deakin.edu.au/index.php/jtlge/article/view/1036/1415

Miro. (2022a). *Introducing Miro concept map.* https://miro.com/aq/ps/concept-map/

Miro. (2022b). *IDOARRT: Lead effective meetings.* https://miro.com/miroverse/idoarrt-lead-effective-meetings/

Miro. (2022c). *Hybrid collaboration field guide.* https://miro.com/blog/hybrid-collaboration-field-guide/

Molenda, M. (2015). In search of the elusive ADDIE model: Performance improvement. *Performance Improvement, 54*(2), 40–42. https://doi.org/10.1002/pfi.21461

Moodle. (2022). *Moodle open-source learning system.* https://moodle.org/

Morin, R. (2016). First Nations instructional leadership for the 21st century. *SELU Research Review Journal, 1*(2), 61–72.

Mount Royal University. (2022). Subject guides. https://library.mtroyal.ca/subjects

MS Teams. (2022). *Microsoft Teams group chat software.* https://www.microsoft.com/en-ca/microsoft-teams/group-chat-software

Mulford, B., Kendall, D., Edmunds, B., Kendall, L., Ewington, J., & Silins, H. (2007). Successful school leadership: What is it and who decides? *Australian Journal of Education, 51*(3), 228–246. https://doi.org/10.1177/000494410705100302

Novak, G., Patterson, E. T., Gavrin, A. D., & Christian, W. (1999). *Just-in-time teaching: Blending active learning with web technology.* Prentice Hall.

Novak, J. D., & Cañas, A. J. (2008). The theory underlying concept maps and how to construct and use them. Technical Report IHMC CmapTools Rev 01–2008. *Florida Institute for Human and Machine Cognition.* http://cmap.ihmc.us/docs/pdf/TheoryUnderlyingConceptMaps.pdf

Onodipe, G., & Ayadi, M. F. (2020). Using smartphones for formative assessment in the flipped classroom. *Journal of Instructional Pedagogies, 23,* 1–20. https://www.aabri.com/manuscripts/193065.pdf

Padlet. (2022). *Padlet.* https://padlet.com/

Palalas, A., Karakanta, C., Mavraki, A., Drampala, K., & Krassa, A. (2020). Mindfulness practices in online learning: Supporting learner self-regulation. *The Journal of Contemplative Inquiry, 7*(1), 247–278.

Pappas, C. (2014, June 14). Instructional design models and theories: Inquiry-based learning model. *eLearning Industry.* https://elearningindustry.com/inquiry-based-learning-model

Parrott, H. M., & Cherry, E. (2011). Using structured reading groups to facilitate deep learning. *Teaching Sociology, 39*(4), 354–370. https://journals.sagepub.com/doi/10.1177/0092055X11418687

Pedaste, M., Mäeots, M., Siiman, L. A., de Jong, T., van Riesen, S. A. N., Kamp, E. T., Manoli, C. C., Zacharia, Z. C., & Eleftheria Tsourlidaki, E. (2015). Phases of inquiry-based learning: Definitions and the inquiry cycle. *Educational Research Review, 14,* 47–61. https://doi.org/10.1016/j.edurev.2015.02.003

Peergrade. (2022). *Peergrade online platform.* https://www.peergrade.io/

Pelaez, N. (2002). Problem-based writing with peer review improves academic performance in physiology. *Advances in Physiology Education, 26,* 174–184. http://advan.physiology.org/cgi/content/full/26/3/174.

Pelletier, K., Brown, M., Brooks, D. C., McCormack, M., Reeves, J., Arbino, N., Bozkurt, A., Crawford, S., Czerniewicz, L., Gibson, R., Linder, K., Mason, M., & Mondelli, V. (2021). *2021 EDUCAUSE horizon report: teaching and learning edition.* https://library.educause.edu/-/media/files/library/2021/4/2021hrteachinglearning.pdf

Piaget, J. (1975). *The equilibration of cognitive structures: The central problem of intellectual development*. University of Chicago Press.

Picciano, A. G. (2021, May). COVID-19 and higher education's future: Issues of technology and governance. *National Center for the Study of Collective Bargaining in Higher Education and the Professions. 12*(2), 1–13. https://thekeep.eiu.edu/jcba/vol12/iss1/2/

Pischetola, M. (2021, September 30). Teaching novice teachers to enhance learning in the hybrid university. *Postdigital Science and Education, 4*, 70–92. https://doi.org/10.1007/s42438-021-00257-1

Plante, K., & Asselin, M. E. (2014). Best practices for creating social presence and caring behaviors online. *Nursing Education Perspectives, 35*(4), 219–223. https://doi.org/10.5480/13-1094.1

Poll Everywhere. (2022). *Poll everywhere*. https://www.polleverywhere.com/

Pond, W. K. (2002, Summer). Distributed education in the 21st century: Implications for quality assurance. *Online Journal of Distance Learning Administration, 5*(2), 1–7 https://ojdla.com/archive/summer52/pond52.pdf

Popplet. (2022). *Popplet for education*. https://www.popplet.com/

Price, E., Goldberg, F., Robinson, S., & McKean, M. (2016). Validity of peer grading using calibrated peer review in a guided-inquiry, conceptual physics course. *Physical Review Physics Education Research, 2*(2), 1–12. https://journals.aps.org/prper/abstract/10.1103/PhysRevPhysEducRes.12.020145

Primera. (2019). Give voice to your students—Use world café. *Primera Courses: Fostering Changes*. https://www.erasmuspluscourses.com/blog/give-voice-to-your-students-use-world-cafe

Ramsden, P. (2003). *Learning to teach in higher education* (2nd ed.). Routledge.

Reeves, T. C. (2000). Alternative assessment approaches for online learning environments in higher education. *Journal of Educational Computing Research, 23*(1), 101–111. https://doi.org/10.2190/GYMQ-78FA-WMTX-J06C

Research Initiative for Teaching Effectiveness. (2022). RITE services. *University of Central Florida*. https://digitallearning.ucf.edu/impact-evaluation/rite-services/

Rourke, L., & Anderson, T. (2002). Using peer teams to lead online discussions. *Journal of Interactive Media in Education, 1* (2002) 1–21. https://jime.open.ac.uk/articles/10.5334/2002-1

Ryan, T. (2021). Designing video feedback to support the socioemotional aspects of online learning. *Education Technology and Research Development, 69*, 137–140. https://doi.org/10.1007/s11423-020-09918-7

Sá, M. J., & Serpa, S. (2020). The COVID-19 pandemic as an opportunity to foster the sustainable development of teaching in higher education. *Sustainability, 12*(20), 2–16. https://www.mdpi.com/2071-1050/12/20/8525

Salhab, R., Hashaykeh, S., Najjar, E., Wahbeh, D., Affouneh, S., & Khlaif, Z. (2021). A proposed ethics code for online learning during crisis. *International Journal of Emerging Technologies in Learning, 16*(20), 238–254. https://online-journals.org/index.php/i-jet/article/view/24735

Salzer, R. (2018). Smartphones as audience response systems for lectures and seminars. *Analytical and Bioanalytical Chemistry, 410*, 1609–1613. https://doi.org/10.1007/s00216-017-0794-8

Sanchez, C. E., Atkinson, K. M., Koenka, A. C., Moshontz, H., & Cooper, H. (2017). Self-grading and peer-grading for formative and summative assessments in 3rd through 12th grade classrooms: A meta-analysis. *Journal of Educational Psychology, 109*(8), 1049–1066. https://doi.org/10.1037/edu0000190

Sands, P. (2002). Inside outside, upside downside: Strategies for connecting online and face-to-face instruction in hybrid courses. *Teaching with Technology Today, 8*(6). 13–21.

Sanford, K., Williams, L., Hopper, T., & McGregor, C. (2012). *Indigenous principles informing teacher education: What we have learned.* In Education, 18(2), 1–12.

Schein, E. J. (2011). The concept of organizational culture: Why bother? In J. M. Shafritz, J. S. Ott, & Y. S. Jang (Eds.), *Classics of organization theory* (7th ed., pp. 349–358). Wadsworth.

Schoology Exchange. (2017). Learning from failure: 6 short edtech case studies you need to read. https://www.schoology.com/blog/learning-failure-6-short-edtech-case-studies-you-need-read

Schrage, M. (1995). *No more teams: Mastering the dynamics of creative collaboration.* Currency Doubleday.

Senge, P. (1990). *The fifth discipline: The art and practice of the learning organization.* Doubleday.

Shanker, S. (2014). *Broader measures for success: Social/emotional learning.* Measuring what Matters, People for Education. https://peopleforeducation.ca/wp-content/uploads/2017/06/MWM-Social-Emotional-Learning.pdf

Shea, P., Li, C. S., Swan, K., & Pickett, A. (2005). Developing learning community in online asynchronous college courses: The role of teaching presence. *The Journal of Asynchronous Learning Networks, 9*(4), 59–82.

Shea, P., Vickers, J., & Hayes, S. (2010). Online instructional effort measured through the lens of teaching presence in the community of inquiry framework: A re-examination of measures and approach. *The International Review of Research in Open and Distance Learning, 11*(3). 127–154. https://www.irrodl.org/index.php/irrodl/article/view/915

Singapore Management University. (2022). The SMU challenge (previously ACE). https://accountancy.smu.edu.sg/accounting-challenge-ace

Sketchboard. (2022). *Sketchboard virtual whiteboard.* https://sketchboard.io/

Skibba, K., & Widmer, M. (2021). Blended faculty community of inquiry transforms online teaching perceptions and practices. In C. Dziuban, C. Graham, A. G. Picciano, & P. D. Moskal (Eds.), *Research perspectives in blended learning (3rd ed.)* (pp. 93–126). Routledge, Taylor and Francis.

Skrypnyk, O., Joksimović, S., Kovanović, V., Dawson, S., Gašević, D., & Siemens, G. (2015). The history and state of blended learning. In G. Siemens, D. Gašević, & S. Dawson (Eds.), *Preparing for the digital university: A review of the history and current state of distance, blended, and online learning* (pp. 55–92). Athabasca University Press.

Slido. (2022). *Polling application.* https://www.sli.do/

Smadi, O., Chamberlain, D., Shifaza, F., & Hamiduzzaman, M. (2021a). Fast and furious shift to online education requires pedagogy transformation. *Australian Nursing and Midwifery Journal, 27*(5), 47–49.

Smadi, O., Chamberlain, D., Shifaza, F., & Hamiduzzaman, M. (2021b). Factors affecting the adoption of the community of inquiry framework in Australian online nursing education: A transition theory perspective. *Nurse Education in Practice, 55* (August), 37–54. https://doi.org/10.1016/j.nepr.2021.103166

Smart Sparrow. (2022). What is learning design? https://www.smartsparrow.com/what-is-learning-design/

Sobhanzadeh, M., & Zizler, P. (2021). Selective assessment in introductory physics labatorials. *The Physics Teacher, 59*, 114–116. https://doi.org/10.1119/10.0003465

Stockdale, D., Parsons, J., & Beauchamp, L. (2013). Instructional leadership in First Nations schools. *Canadian Journal of Native Education, 36*(1), 95–149.

SurveyMonkey. (2022). *SurveyMonkey*. https://www.surveymonkey.com/

Taghizade, A., Hatami, J., Noroozi, O., Farrokhnia, M., & Hassanzadeh, A. (2020). Fostering learners' perceived presence and high-level learning outcomes in online learning environments. *Education Research International, 2020*, Article ID 6026231, 1–9. https://doi.org/10.1155/2020/6026231

Taylor Institute. (2022). Learning module: Critical reflection. https://taylorinstitute.ucalgary.ca/resources/module/critical-reflection

Teaching Learning Support Services. (2016). Report on the blended learning initiative. *University of Ottawa*. https://saea-tlss.uottawa.ca/en/innovation-research/strategic-research-impact-assessment/initiatives-implemented

TED-Ed. (2022). How do I create TED-Ed lessons? https://help.ted.com/hc/en-us/articles/360005307714-How-to-create-a-TED-Ed-Lesson

Thaler, R., & Sunstein, C. (2008). *Nudge*. Penguin Books.

Theodora, R. (2019). Five reasons why you should love group work. *Ontario Tech University*. https://blog.ontariotechu.ca/five-reasons-why-you-should-love-group-work

Thistlethwaite, J. (2006). More thoughts on "assessment drives learning." *Medical Education, 40*(11), 1149–1150.

Thomas, C., & Brown, B. (2021). Formative assessment strategies to support group work. *Education in the North, 28*(2), 134–155. https://www.abdn.ac.uk/education/research/eitn/journal/653/

Torras, M. E., & Mayordomo, R. (2011). Teaching presence and regulation in an electronic portfolio. *Computers in Human Behavior, 27*, 2284–2291.

Toulouse, P. (2016). *What matters in Indigenous education: Implementing a vision committed to holism, diversity and engagement*. People for Education.

Tuckman, B. W. (1965). Developmental sequence in small groups. *Psychological Bulletin, 63*(6), 384–399.

Twigg, C. A. (2003). Improving quality and reducing costs: Designs for effective learning. *Change, 35*(4), 23–29.

University of Arizona. (2022). Writing an article critique. https://writingcenter.uagc.edu/writing-article-critique

University of Calgary. (2022). Blended and online learning resources. https://taylorinstitute.ucalgary.ca/resources/blended-online-learning

University of California Los Angeles. (2019). Calibrated peer review tool. http://cpr.molsci.ucla.edu/Home

University of Central Florida. (2022). Blended learning toolkit. https://
blended.online.ucf.edu/2011/06/07/building-your-course/

University of Ottawa. (2022) Blended tool box. https://saea-tlss.uottawa.ca/
en/teaching-technologies/documentation/teaching-technologies

University of Waterloo. (2022a). Concept mapping tools. https://uwaterloo
.ca/centre-for-teaching-excellence/teaching-resources/teaching-tips/
teaching-tips-educational-technologies/all/concept-mapping-tools

University of Waterloo. (2022b). Making group contracts. https://uwaterloo
.ca/centre-for-teaching-excellence/teaching-resources/teaching-tips/
developing-assignments/group-work/making-group-contracts

University of Western Ontario. (2022). Western active learning spaces
(WALS). https://wals.uwo.ca/

University of Wisconsin—Madison. (2022). Blended learning toolkit. https://
blendedtoolkit.wisc.edu/design/

University of Wisconsin—Stout. (2022). Creating and using rubrics for
assessment. https://www.uwstout.edu/academics/online-distance
-education/online-professional-development/educational-resources
-rubrics/creating-and-using-rubrics-assessment

Vaughan, N. D. (2010). A blended community of inquiry approach: Linking
student engagement to course redesign. *Internet and Higher Education,
13*(1–2), 60–65.

Vaughan, N. D. (2013). Investigating how digital technologies can support
a triad-approach to assessment in higher education. *Canadian Journal of
Learning and Technology, 39*(3), 1–22. https://www.cjlt.ca/index.php/cjlt/
article/view/26309

Vaughan, N. D. (2014). Student engagement and blended learning: Making
the assessment connection. *Education Sciences, 4*(4), 247–264. http://www
.mdpi.com/2227-7102/4/4/247

Vaughan, N. D., Cleveland-Innes, M., & Garrison, D. R. (2013). *Teaching
in blended learning environments: Creating and sustaining communities of
inquiry.* Athabasca University Press. https://www.aupress.ca/books/120229
-teaching-in-blended-learning-environments/

Vaughan, N. D., & Garrison, D. R. (2005). Creating cognitive presence in a
blended faculty development community. *Internet and Higher Education,
8*(1), 1–12.

Vaughan, N. D., & Garrison, D. R. (2006). A blended faculty community of inquiry: Linking leadership, course redesign and evaluation. *Canadian Journal of University Continuing Education, 32*(2), 67–92.

Vaughan, N. D., & Lee Wah, J. (2020). Community of inquiry: Future practical directions—shared metacognition. *International Journal of E-Learning and Distance Education*, special issue on *Technology and Teacher Education, 35*(1). 1–25. http://www.ijede.ca/index.php/jde/article/view/1154

Vimeo. (2022). *Livestream video application.* https://livestream.com/

Waghid, Z., Meda, L., & Chiroma, J. A. (2021). Assessing cognitive, social and teaching presences during emergency remote teaching at a South African university. *International Journal of Information and Learning Technology, 38*(5), 413–432. https://doi.org/10.1108/IJILT-01-2021-0006

Weebly. (2022). *Create your own website.* https://www.weebly.com/

Wiggins, G., & McTighe, J. (1998). Backward design. In G. Wiggins & J. McTighe (Eds.) *Understanding by design* (pp. 13–34). Association for Supervision and Curriculum Development (ASCD).

Wiliam, D., & Leahy, S. (2015). *Embedding formative assessment: Practical techniques for K12 classrooms.* Learning Sciences.

Wilson, E. O. (2012). *The social conquest of Earth.* W.W. Norton.

Wise, A. (2020). Online discussion student facilitation guidelines. *Harmonize.* https://info.42lines.net/online-discussion-student-facilitation-guidelines-drwise

Wix. (2022). *Free website builder.* https://www.wix.com/

Wolf, E. (2010). *Europe and the people without history.* University of California Press.

Woolley, A., Malone, T. W., & Chabris, W. (2015, January 15). Why some teams are smarter than others. *The New York Times, 5.* https://www.nytimes.com/2015/01/18/opinion/sunday/why-some-teams-are-smarter-than-others.html

WordPress. (2022). *WordPress.* https://wordpress.com/

World Café Conversations. (2022). The world café: Shaping our futures through conversations that matter. http://www.theworldcafe.com/

Yang, M., & Carless, D. (2013). The feedback triangle and the enhancement of dialogic feedback processes. *Teaching in Higher Education, Critical Perspectives, 18*(3), 285–297. https://doi.org/10.1080/13562517.2012.719154

Yeh, S. S. (2009). The cost-effectiveness of raising teacher quality. *Educational Research Review, 4*(3), 220–232.

YouTube. (2022). *YouTube video sharing application.* https://www.youtube.com/

Yu, Z., Li, M. (2022). A bibliometric analysis of community of inquiry in online learning contexts over twenty-five years. *Education and Information Technologies 27,* 11669–11688. https://doi.org/10.1007/s10639-022-11081-w

Zhang, H., Lin, L., Zhan, Y., & Youqun Ren, Y. (2016). The impact of teaching presence on online engagement behaviors. *Journal of Educational Computing Research, 54*(7), 887–900.

Zhao, H., & Sullivan, K. P. H. (2017). Teaching presence in computer conferencing learning environments: Effects on interaction, cognition and learning uptake. *British Journal of Educational Technology, 48*(2), 538–551.

Zoom. (2022). *Zoom web-conferencing application.* https://zoom.us